DIALOGUE

The Influence of Intra-personal Discourse on Interpersonal Communication in Fostering Relationships in a Digital Age

EMMANUEL OLUSOLA

 FriesenPress

Suite 300 - 990 Fort St
Victoria, BC, V8V 3K2
Canada

www.friesenpress.com

Foreword: Rev. Fr. Anthony Eseke, PhD
Assistant Professor of Communication & Public Relations
Messiah University, Pennsylvania, United States

ISBN
978-1-03-910361-0 (Hardcover)
978-1-03-910360-3 (Paperback)
978-1-03-910362-7 (eBook)

1. LANGUAGE ARTS & DISCIPLINES, COMMUNICATION STUDIES

Distributed to the trade by The Ingram Book Company

TABLE OF CONTENTS

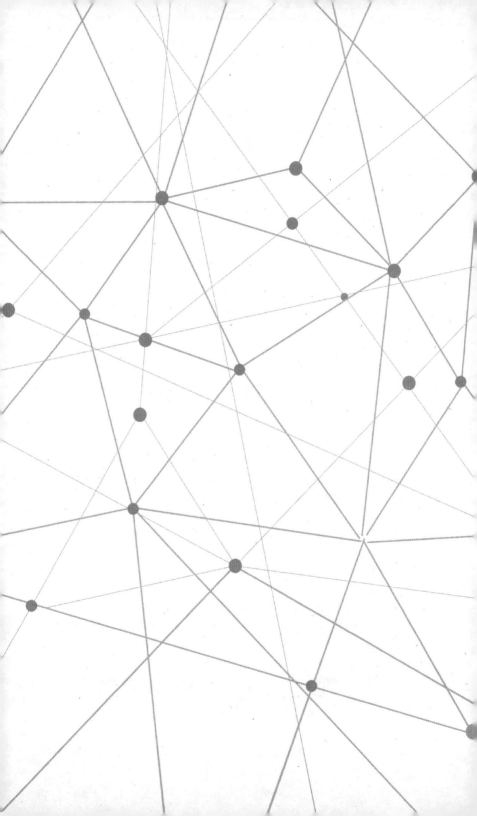

Nihil Obstat

Rev. Fr. Victor Abimbola Amole, PhD

Imprimatur

Most Rev. Dr. Gabriel 'Leke Abegunrin
Archbishop of the Roman Catholic
Archdiocese of Ibadan
Ibadan, Oyo State, Nigeria

DEDICATION

———•———

To the glory of God, this book is dedicated

To

All who heed the voice of their inner discourse
and allow this to positively influence their
dialogue with others.

and to

All those who have accompanied me
in 20 years of priestly ministry and
my academic pursuits.

ACKNOWLEDGEMENTS

———•———

I believe the two most important words, which open doors and bring more favors, are "thank you". A grateful heart enables one to receive more than what has already been given. On this note, I wish to express my sentiments of appreciation to the author of life, God almighty, who gave me everything needed to begin and complete this project. It is indeed God's voice that echoes in every human heart as He engages us in inner dialogues as we carry out daily activities, build relationships, and foster peaceful co-existence. To him be all honor and glory.

God did not create humans in a vacuum; He endowed us with the gift of family. The family is the bedrock and foundation of every individual. My worldview continues to be shaped by every member of my biological family – OLUSOLA. For this, I am eternally grateful to my parents, especially my mum, Mrs. V. M. Olusola, whose encouraging words and prayers urge me on. To my siblings, I cannot thank you enough for what you are to me, and I pray to God to bless you all. My little angels (nephews and nieces) mean the world to me, and the wisdom I see in you all during our small talks is priceless. May you all continue to grow in favor with God and humanity.

To my religious family, I am very grateful to my Local Ordinary, Archbishop Gabriel Leke Abegunrin, who has been a pillar of support in many ways and who also graciously granted the Imprimatur to this publication. May the good Lord continue to be your strength as you shepherd us. In a similar token, I am thankful to Most Rev. Felix Alaba A. Job (Emeritus Archbishop of Ibadan), the priests, the religious and laity in the Roman Catholic archdiocese of Ibadan. Thank you to all.

Over the last few years, I have been working in the Roman Catholic diocese of Saskatoon, Saskatchewan, Canada. I thank Most Rev. Donald Bolen (Archbishop of Regina) who, as Bishop of Saskatoon invited and welcomed me to Saskatoon and who also wrote the first blurb for this book. My appreciation also goes to Most Rev. Mark Hagemoen, the incumbent Bishop of Saskatoon and the priests of the diocese. My stay in Saskatchewan has been gratifying thanks to the people of God in the Trinity of Parishes where I have been privileged to serve as pastor – St. Aloysius, Allan; St. Mary, Colonsay; and St. Alphonse, Viscount, Saskatchewan. In these years, we have endeavored to build a community of "All for One and One for All". I sincerely thank you all. The same sentiments go to the teachers and students of Bethlehem and Bishop Murray High Schools, Saskatoon, where I have been chaplain for the last five years.

My litany of appreciation would not be complete without acknowledging everyone who has been of assistance to me in the last 20 years of my priestly ministry. In both my pastoral and academic assignments, I have encountered people in various parts of Africa, Europe, and North America, whose worldviews shaped mine in many ways and whose experiences greatly informed this book. I have also received the support of many that limitation of space here will not allow me to mention by name. You know yourselves, and God, who knows the assistance you have rendered to me these years, will richly reward you. To my friends – priests, religious and lay faithful, I thank you for being there through the thick and thin over these years. May the good Lord continue to keep us united as we work together to build better relationships through effective dialogue.

In summary, special thanks to everyone who helped shape this publication. I sincerely thank Margaret Sanche, the Archivist for the Roman Catholic Diocese of Saskatoon, Saskatchewan, who, with an eagle eye approach, proofread this book's manuscript. The same thanks go to Rev. Fr. Prof. Anthony Eseke, who wrote the book's foreword, Rev. Fr. Victor Amole, PhD, who granted the Nihil Obstat, and Rev. Fr. Gerald Musa, PhD, who wrote the second blurb for this publication. To everyone else who may not have been mentioned here by name, I thank you all and I pray to God to bless you abundantly.

Fr. Emmanuel Olusola, PhD
(Fr. Supreem)
olummacy@yahoo.com

FOREWORD

———●———

Communication Studies, as we know it today, became an independent field through the social sciences. Consequently, the scientific method became the dominant mode of inquiry in Communication Studies. Like most sciences, Communication values observation, experimentation, and verifiability. It also values replication, measurability, and universalizability. The challenge, however, to the scientific mode of inquiry is that discourses on "intra-personal" and "spiritual communication" may be ignored because the "spiritual" is not easily measurable.

In this book, *Dialogue: The Influence of Intra-personal Discourse on Interpersonal Communication in Fostering Relationships in a Digital Age*, Dr. Olusola attempts a commendable exploration of spiritual and psychological influences in human communication. His overarching thesis is borne out of scripture that: "A good person out of the store of goodness in his heart produces good... for of the fullness of the heart the mouth speaks" (Luke 6:45). In his analysis of the subject matter, Fr. Olusola nicely weaves his childhood stories and motivating testimonies from two decades of priestly ministry. He masterfully uses grand-narratives and meta-narratives from the Christian and the Yoruba traditions to create useful contexts for discussing cultural dialogues.

Fr. Olusola clearly demonstrates his mastery of communication science, especially communication as a system; where conflicts and miscommunications create tensions that only genuine dialogue and communication can restore the social homeostasis. Among others, the book presents practical ways to manage conflicts and increase listening effectiveness and skills for attaining authentic dialogue. Combining experiences as a pastor and years of academic pursuit, he makes the case that we earnestly need dialogue in our individual minds and souls, and in our families and cultures. Such dialogues, however, begin with a multidimensional approach to communication – sort of a dialogue with God, a dialogue with nature, a dialogue with self, a dialogue with humanity, and a dialogue with technology (Mowlana, 2018). It is through these ways that relationships are built and sustained.

More importantly, getting to this highly desired multidimensional approach to communication begins with reading this book. Contextualizing the thesis of this book within the ambient of the digital age, he explores how modern and traditional forms of communication can borrow from the good aspects of each other in fostering human relationships. Fr. Olusola crafts this book in an easy-to-read format and, since the issue of dialogue permeates every sphere of human life, this contribution to the science of communication should find a place in the home, offices, and all other contexts where people desire peaceful co-existence.

I say without mincing words that there is no better time for this publication than our present socio-political and cultural milieu, and I recommend this book to anyone who desires enduring relationships and peaceful co-existence borne out of authentic dialogue. In sum, if there is a book that needs to be not just in your library, but most importantly in your hands, that book is: *Dialogue: The Influence of Intra-personal Discourse on Interpersonal Communication in Fostering Relationships in a Digital Age.*

Rev. Fr. Anthony Eseke, Ph.D.
Assistant Professor of Communication & Public Relations
Messiah University
Pennsylvania, United States

INTRODUCTION

———●———

Everyday life is replete with various activities and events – births/ deaths, peace/war, accords/misunderstandings, to mention just a few. All of us, at various times, have been involved in one or more of these events that form the reality of human existence. At the root of these activities is communication, which undergirds and shapes every human action. Everyday activities, guided by communication, help to form and maintain relationships. To a great extent, the negative dimensions of daily experiences stem from the inability of humans to engage in effective communication in the form of dialogue with one another, whether as individuals or as a group of nations. The adverse effects of this on individuals, families, and society as a whole can only be imagined.

I am always intrigued each time I watch debates in the parliaments of democratic nations around the world and see the manner with which people in power dialogue with one another. From the awe-inspiring House of Commons in London to the ancient halls of Parliament in Rome; from the cradle of modern democracy in Washington DC and the House of Commons in Ottawa to Nigeria's nascent democratic government's National Assembly in Abuja or the more recent democracy in South Africa with its National Assembly in Cape Town, the same drama unfolds as people often engage in shouting matches in an attempt to make their opinions heard over and above those of others. Some even go beyond shouting down opposing views to actual engagement in fistfights. We have all been awed at some point as we see punches and other objects flying around the hallowed chambers of some law-making houses.

What occurs in the high echelons of governance is replicated among groups of friends and in many homes, offices, and even places of worship. I have heard stories of how many husbands or wives become agitated each time one says to the other, "We need to talk." To avoid the much-needed dialogue in many homes, it has been said that the husband or wife stays out late into the night only to return when the spouse should be asleep. In other instances, the spouse who is told there is need for conversation confronts the person asking to talk in such a hostile manner that the latter drops the idea as if it were a hot potato. A great number of problems that might have been nipped in the bud have been allowed to escalate into bigger issues because people avoided the all-important conversation – dialogue!

Humanity has arrived, sadly so, at a point in history where we find it hard to engage in civil conversations and share ideas in a way to arrive at a compromise. Caution is thrown into the wind each time the idea of arriving at what is mutually beneficial to everyone is mentioned, since each one sees his or her idea as the best that must prevail. Dialogue, which sustained the ancient Greco-Roman society thereby enabling people in those times to reason together and excel in the field of arts, philosophy, medicine, to mention but a few, continues to elude us in our present dispensation.

One of the main discoveries of the human person is the ability to communicate. The word "communication" comes from the Latin root *communicare*, which can be divided into two parts: *commune* and *are*. The former means "together", while the latter means to "have". As such, *communicare* can be literally translated to mean "having together or sharing together". Since communication has to do with sharing together, dialogue is an essential aspect of this sharing since, through dialogue, diverse ideas are espoused towards arriving at a common goal and peaceful coexistence. In ancient times, communication went above a way of arriving at a common goal since people invented verbal and non-verbal cues to make sense of their environments and survive in their habitat.

Dialogue entails how people use these cues in understanding not just their own positions but also the points of view of other persons. Although some persons limit dialogue to what happens when two persons engage in communication, this book argues that dialogue begins with the individual. It is the form of communication that occurs within each person, and it influences how we relate with people around us. This is known in communication scholarship as intra-personal dialogue. It is the inner communication from which other forms of communication stem.

The importance of the inner dimension of communication cannot be over-emphasized; however, many factors condition this inner dialogue, which everyone engages in on a daily basis, sometimes without even knowing it. Oftentimes, our minds are so crowded that we do not have a good dialogue within us, and this is reflected in the way we treat people around us. There is therefore need for us to calm our inner self and allow this conversation to take place from time to time. Let me use the analogy of an experience I had many years ago, growing up in Nigeria, to buttress this point.

In those times, we usually experienced the dry season between the months of October to March. As such, since there was little or no water supply from the city's water corporation, many families dug wells within their compounds. These wells dried up in the aforementioned dry season months, making people scramble to get water from streams or wells of neighbors who lived close to a waterbed. It became a competition to get up early in the morning to arrive at the well in good time if you wanted to get clean water. As the day wore on and many people made their way to the well, the water got muddy, and after been fetched by many people, even dried up only to spring up again after some period of locking up the well. At times, the well was locked till the next day, so as to allow the water to spring up in a large quantity.

One of the things that intrigued my young but curious mind on those voyages to the well was the ability to see a reflection of myself in the clear water each time we went to the well early enough. However, each time we went late to the well, the water got muddy and nothing was seen but brown water. As such, I made it a point of duty to wake my siblings early in the morning so that we got to the well before others. The very early morning look into the deep well gave a wonderful image of anyone looking down into the water because the water was still and undisturbed at that time.

Much later, through studies and other life experiences, I came to understand that the human mind is like that little experiment I carried out around the well as a young boy. The human mind is able to achieve so much if left unencumbered by all the noise we have in our present hyper-technological civilization. Dialogue becomes more positive and rewarding if the mind is settled and able to consider different options so as to make an informed choice. This does not only affect the person making the choice, but the other persons he or she relates with in the course of that day.

Although some scholars argue, based on its Latin root, *dialogos,* and the prefix *dia,* that dialogue must necessarily involve two persons, this book focuses not just on the prefix but takes both terms in their entirety with an emphasis on *logos.* That is, granted that the term *logos* can be translated to mean "word", it doesn't need two parties to exist. The "word" exists within each individual as ideas, irrespective of any external factor. As such, a great deal of conversation occurs within the individual, and this affects how he or she relates to the outside world.

This inner conversation is called intra-personal communication with a robust effect on the interpersonal communication, which has to do with communication with other persons. This book focuses on these two levels of communication while presenting other factors that enhance or inhibit dialogue in our present society. It is expected that this effort will resurrect a robust appreciation of dialogue within the reader that will snowball into building an effective communication with others, thereby bringing about a more peaceful world order.

A number of studies have examined the connection between what happens in the intra-personal discourse, interpersonal dialogue, and everyday life (Clarke, et al., 2005; Step & Finucane, 2002). In a study among young children in Alberta, Canada, Brooks (2005) examines the import of interpersonal communication and intra-personal dialogue in construction of knowledge. This was done using the activity of drawing in a classroom to affirm how both the intra-personal and interpersonal aspects of communication influence one another. This study centered on the issue of light, as the children were asked to draw a flashlight based on their past experience of light and darkness.

Brooks encouraged the children to form their questions and investigate their thoughts either in small groups or as individuals. As such, each child drew from past experiences of flashlights they had at home, but such experiences were fine-tuned as they looked at the drawings of their peers. The drawing was said not only to be generative, but also the difference between each subsequent drawing showed a transformation from previously held ideas (intra-personal) based on the interpersonal knowledge shared with others in the class, which affected each child's intra-personal dialogue.

Brooks thus affirms that: "The drawings provided a common point of reference that was shared among the children, and were examples of new knowledge existing in a shared context" (2005:83). Through drawing, these children made visible their inner ideas and thoughts. In fact, some of the children worked in groups of two, whereby the thoughts of each influenced the other and, through interpersonal sharing, they both came up with a better idea of what a flashlight should look like. Brooks concludes, "The interpersonal level could be viewed as the foundation from which the intra-personal level grows ... It is at this time that children's ideas, questions, and misconceptions are most visible" (2005:86).

This present book deviates from the study by Brooks, however. Instead of seeing interpersonal communication as the basis for intra-personal dialogue, the thesis of this book is that the intra-personal level is the base upon which all that happens in the interpersonal level is formed and shaped. This is because it is at this level that ideas and opinions, sometimes based on past experiences or present realities, are formed, which goes a long way in influencing how one operates on the interpersonal and other levels of communication.

Every human history is a composite of an examination of the past, juxtaposing it with the present so as to chart a better path for the future. A great number of feats accomplished by humans have been made possible by examining historical facts and making the best of such facts. The present effort of writing this book is borne out of my experience as a Roman Catholic priest for the last 20 years. I had the privilege of being ordained a Catholic priest on July 14, 2001, along with six other deacons (Joseph Akanbi, Michael Domingo, Anthony Adeola, Joachim Akee, Gabriel Anekwe, and John Uzoagba of blessed memory) at St. Mary's Cathedral, Ibadan, by Most Rev. Felix Alaba Job, emeritus Archbishop of Ibadan.

From my first pastoral placement at St. Mary Cathedral, Oke Padre, Ibadan, to many places in Europe and North America that I have been privileged to exercise my priestly ministry in the last 20 years, dialogue and communication with God's people both in the academic and faith communities have helped to shape my worldview. In the academic field, I have had the opportunity of lecturing in a number of universities. Presently, my engagement in full-time pastoral duties has enabled me to further study human relationships within the parish setting and to connect my present experiences with my studies in the field of human and group communication. This book is a product of the synergy of both my pastoral and academic experiences.

In tandem with Systems Theory, which this book employs as its theoretical base, my encounters with people across cultures and places show that human experience is the same across the globe and that it is the same aspiration that fuels the passion of all, albeit with unique contextualizations. At the threshold of writing this book, as I engage in dialogue with the people of God in the Archdiocese of Ibadan, currently with Archbishop Gabriel Leke Abegunrin as our Chief Shepherd, I see a people who, formed by the African culture of fellow feeling, strive to build strong relationships and support one another through every phase of life.

In my dialogue with students in the various citadels of learning where I have taught, I always endeavored to make the classroom an avenue for cross-pollination of ideas. Following the thoughts of Paolo Freire, I have written in academic journals to oppose the

"Banking System" of education through which students merely regurgitate whatever the lecturer teaches. Instead, I am a supporter of the participatory learning method, which brings everyone into a new level of knowledge through dialogue. As such, through dialogue and sharing, it is always intriguing to see how the experience of one student reinforces and enhances the academic pursuit of another.

In my pastoral placement in Saskatchewan, Canada over the last 5 years, I have met people (mostly farmers) who not only taught me about the dialogue that should exist between persons and their environment, but also the fact that dialogue in shared faith experiences helps people to nurture one another. It is therefore based on these different experiences that I decided to embark on this project as a fruit of research in human communication and in thanksgiving to God for the last 20 years of having the privilege of sharing in the priesthood according to the order of Melchizedek.

Consequently, apart from this introductory section, which succinctly highlights how this book unfolds, the book is divided into six chapters. The first chapter examines the concept of dialogue. Here, many aspects of dialogue from the scientific, cultural, and religious dimensions are examined. The main gist here is that dialogue is seen in every aspect of human life and it is dialogue that sustains relationships and the entire human community. In the second chapter, the book presents its theoretical orientation in the Systems Theory.

Although Systems Theory originated from the biological sciences, it has been employed in the social sciences to explain phenomena in family communication. Also examined under this chapter are Functional Theory and Symbolic Convergence, both of which further explain the Systems Theory in showing how things are connected in nature and how, through a process of interdependence and sharing of the same symbols in communication, equilibrium that sustains the system is maintained through feedback. The chapter affirms that feedback is an essential aspect of dialogue and every communication process.

The third chapter looks at listening as an important dimension of dialogue. It affirms the need to pay attention to those inner cues (intra-personal factors) that affect the external actions (interpersonal communication). In doing so, this chapter shows that listening is not limited to verbal communication, but that a great deal of communication occurs at the non-verbal level and that the ability to listen also shows how effective one is in the dialogue process. While some regard listening as a simple act, this chapter shows that, in actual fact, great effort is required to be an effective listener. This effort enables the receiver of a communication message to give appropriate feedback to the source of the message. The chapter presents the different stages of the listening process and how one can improve listening effectiveness. The chapter affirms that no one can actively engage in the dialogue process without effective listening.

The crux of the book can be seen in the fourth chapter, which holds that effective interpersonal communication is dependent on efficient intra-personal dialogue. Here, it is argued that past experiences, present situations, future expectations, and many factors occur within the human person that affect how he or she relates on the interpersonal level. It is said here that no one comes to a dialogue process *tabula rasa*, that is, empty. Everyone comes with a baggage of factors that affects how one processes ideas internally before they are manifested externally through interpersonal communication. Citing academic articles and real life experiences, this chapter shows how these two levels of communication are not just interconnected but that intra-personal dialogue also influences interpersonal communication.

The effort of this publication would not be complete without a critical look at dialogue with reference to the present digital age and how this continues to shape human existence. As such, chapter five of the book highlights this phenomenon by citing the importance of the digital age, but at the same time, notes the adverse effects of the wrong use of social media with regards to dialogue. Many persons, hiding behind computer screens or other forms of new media, have created the kind of dialogues that have rocked the boat in many spheres of life. The need for the right use of the new media is advocated in this chapter, while at the same time favoring face-to-face traditional means of communication as that through which the emotional dimension of dialogue is taken into consideration and the real idea of communication as a bridge-builder comes to the fore.

The sixth chapter of this book peruses the need to rediscover the importance of dialogue in the present age. As said earlier, a great deal of what is happening in the world today – the wars, the misunderstanding between nations, tension in many homes, etc. – can be traced to inadequate intra-personal dialogue in world leaders or among individual family members, which leads to other problems on the interpersonal level. For instance, what gets camouflaged under the guise of diplomacy between leaders of nations has no such coloration between husbands and wives, parents and children, etc. In most cases, the inability to dialogue on the family level brings about problems that are visible to all in broken marriages or the challenges faced by children in school or other spheres of life.

In the workplace, the inability to manage intra-personal dialogue has resulted in tensions or conflicts among colleagues. There is also the issue of intergenerational situations in which, if dialogue is not well used, misunderstandings can occur between the young and the elderly. In view of all this, and in a bid to restore dialogue to its rightful place in human communication, the concluding chapter of the book emphasizes the need to be cognizant of intra-personal dialogue as a veritable way to building a better world order.

The book concludes with a call for everyone to get involved in this task of giving dialogue its rightful place by avoiding the mistake of looking at communication as a trivial human activity. A better understanding of intra-personal dialogue and its influence on other forms of communication is thus presented as the panacea for a great deal of the challenges human society faces presently. To overcome these challenges, all hands must be on deck as dialogue and communication are given their rightful places in society. Please join me in this excursion into the world of dialogue as we now turn the page to the first chapter of the book.

CHAPTER ONE

---•---

Examining Dialogue:
Concept and Practice

At the first lecture I attended as a Master's student of Communication Studies, one of the things the professor said which has remained with me till date was: "You cannot not communicate." Communication is both an integral and essential aspect of daily life with which humans express themselves, get to know their environment better so as to survive therein, pass information/knowledge from one generation to the next, and shape discourse in their society. One can only imagine how communication, especially the new media, has greatly influenced everything in our society today.

Human society, in which a hundred years ago people moved about on horseback, has witnessed the latest technological advancement in aviation with supersonic jets traveling at unprecedented speed. The landline telephonic means of communication which began with Alexander Graham Bell's invention in 1876 has given way to more effective and portable cellular phones, thanks to satellite technology. Banking and commerce can now be easily done through cell phones, and the sharing of information with people in any part of the world is now done with just a click of the computer mouse.

Indeed, communication has brought about unprecedented changes and development to our world. Although communication is vast with many dimensions, levels, and models, the focus of this book is on dialogue as a vital aspect of communication since it pervades and permeates every phase of human life. On December 18, 2019, the United States House of Representatives voted to impeach the American President, Donald J. Trump, making him the third President to have been impeached in the more than 240 years of American history. Leading to this impeachment vote were debates for and against the same in the various committees of the House of Representatives, among which were the Ways and Means, the Intelligence, and Judiciary Committees, to mention but a few.

Many persons watched around the globe as both Democrat and Republican members of the House of Representatives argued their cases and interrogated witnesses. Although Trump was later acquitted on February 5, 2020, by the Republican-dominated Senate, the intriguing part of this debacle was the kind of dialogue that ensued as people shouted, yelled, and repeated the same points of view, even when such had been debunked by many previous speakers who had offered evidence to back up opposing claims. It got to a point that one of the members of the House pleaded with his colleagues to simply pass if they had nothing new to say other than the repetition of the same points that had been made over and over again by their colleagues. The debates in this House of Representatives, and later on in the United States Senate, show just a glimpse of what happens in many democracies and private homes across the globe.

What occurred in the United States is also seen many times in the United Kingdom or even in Canada as Parliamentarians shout one another down or exhibit a robust display of acceptance or refutation of the claim of other persons in more dramatic ways. There have been moments of "boos" for an opposing view or outbursts of applause for a favored argument in these chambers. In the example of Trump's impeachment mentioned above, one notices that people tended to engage in "dialogue" in a way that shows they have either not listened to previous speakers or they just wish to tenaciously hold to their own beliefs without any show of understanding of someone else's point of view.

The United States is said to be polarized on many fronts at the present time, and this hinders efforts at achieving authentic dialogue, sometimes even among Americans of the same household. The election year of 2020 in the United States witnessed a heightened division among Americans. The emergence of Joseph R. Biden as the flag bearer for the Democratic Party and his choice of Kamala Harris as running mate created divergent points of discourse among Democrats and Republicans alike. The first presidential debate between Donald Trump and Joseph Biden on September 29, 2020 was widely condemned as being everything a dialogue process should not be, since it was marred by interruptions and insults.

The second presidential debate was not held due to the fact that Trump contracted COVID-19 about this time and was hospitalized for a number of days at Walter Reed hospital. As such, the Commission on Presidential debate decided to conduct a virtual debate instead of the traditional in-person version. The Trump campaign declined to participate in the second debate but took part in the third and last debate on October 22, 2020. This was judged to be more dialogical and productive compared to the combative first debate. This political dialogue which occupied many fronts in the United States of America in the four years prior was taken to the polls in the November 3, 2020 election.

After many weeks of counting ballots, President Trump challenged the outcome of the election in various courts, but without any concrete evidence to back up his claim, the courts threw out his petitions. On December 14, 2020, the Electoral College voted and endorsed Biden's victory in the presidential election. However, President Trump continued to claim the election was stolen from him. On January 6, 2021, as United States' legislators, including the Vice President, Mike Pence, gathered at the Capitol to count electoral votes which was the last step towards stamping Joseph Biden's victory, Trump held a rally at the White House where he continued to repeat the claims that the election was rigged.

The whole world watched in shock as Trump's supporters, after listening to his speech at this rally, invaded the citadel of American democracy in a bid to overturn the result of the presidential election. After the mayhem which ensued, 5 persons died included a Capitol police officer while many others sustained various degrees of injury. After the mob attack on the capitol, which many persons called an insurrection, Trump read a speech on teleprompter in which, for the first time, he acknowledged that a new administration will be sworn in on January 6, 2021. The next day, however, he declared he will not be attending Biden's inauguration.

In view of all that happened, the leaders of the Democratic caucus asked Trump to resign or that Vice President Pence should invoke the 25th amendment which will declare Trump unfit to continue in office. There was also the option of impeaching Trump for a second time. Mike Pence did not invoke the 25th amendment and Trump did not resign. At the end, Joseph Biden's administration was inaugurated on January 20, 2021, becoming the 46th President of the United States. The week after this, Trump was impeached for a second time by the House of Representatives only to be acquitted again by the Senate. As the drama which unfolded prior to the inauguration of Biden lingered, many persons wondered, going forward, what moral right the United States of America will have to meddle in democratic affairs around the world?

As can be seen in the result of the elections in the United States, whatever begins as daily conversations and dialogue around dinner tables, on buses, in offices, etc., can have a tremendous effect on the nation at large. Examples of shortcomings in the dialogue format sometimes witnessed in parliaments from the United States and aforementioned major democracies around the world can help us to understand what happens in other aspects of life where dialogue continues to elude people in their dealings with each another. In the episodes cited above, people merely talked, or oftentimes, just talked down to each other without really engaging in dialogue.

Authentic dialogue begins with the ability to have a point of view and at the same time recognize that other people also have viewpoints, that each is entitled to his or her opinion, and that through cross-pollination of ideas, a new understanding might be arrived at that reflects the views of the communicating persons. As I said at the introductory part of this book, my stay in Saskatchewan in the last five years has further taught me that humans can learn so much from nature. An example of this is found in bees. Imagine how bees get honey from flowers without destroying the source of their honey. The bees do this by collecting pollen and nectar as food from flowers.

As the bees do this, they store the nectar in their stomach and pass this from one worker-bee to the other until the water is diminished. It is this nectar that becomes the honey we enjoy. In all this, the bees do not just take what they need from the flower, they also help to cross-pollinate, therefore conserving nature while making something new out of their contact with the flower. In this simple example, we see how the relationship between the bee and flower brings out something new – honey – without any adverse effect on either. It is this collaborative effort that is expected of an effective dialogue.

I once had an experience at a conference where a professor began his presentation by giving us the answers to the questions he wanted to discuss and asking us to brainstorm together to determine what the questions were. In this way, we journeyed from the known to the unknown. This has been referred to as generative dialogue. In this vein, Baraldi sees dialogue as "a form of communication in which participants' positions are intentionally questioned and negotiated (second order positioning), in order to reach their positive interactive and reflexive positioning (2009: 13). The idea of positioning is emphasized to underscore the fact that, in communication process, the parties should make conscious efforts not to be static but make a conscious move by shifting from a previously held position towards the view of the other party.

We also see brainstorming and shifting grounds in that very important aspect of communication that rakes in millions of dollars around the world today – film making. The great movies we enjoy often begin with a simple idea. Scriptwriters gather the production crew to brainstorm and merge together the different pieces of the central idea. There is a lot of give-and-take, fine-tuning, and rejection/affirmation of ideas before the final script is produced. Even in the process of film production, the scenes are not sequential as when we watch the movie. Sometimes, the last scene is shot first because of the availability or lack of actors. At the end of the production stage, through the process of editing, the pieces are then brought together to form a coherent whole.

In the theoretical orientation of Systems Theory, which the book explores in the second chapter, this notion that communication is about give-and-take and an interchange of roles is further elaborated. That is, it is a process whereby one person (the source) who initiates the communication process becomes the receiver of feedback from the other person who was hitherto the receiver, but now the source of the message after having internalized it.

Brief Historical Overview of Dialogue

The academic study of dialogue finds its roots in the philosophical thoughts of Socrates and has been buttressed by his followers Aristotle and Plato in the Greek world, while Cicero's oration holds sway in the Roman universe. Socrates believed people could reason together in the *polis*, which was what their gathering place for discussion at the time was called. It is from the idea of the *polis* that the term politics originated as a way of airing the views of people with regards to how they are to be governed. Socrates' effort at introducing this novelty to Greek society was not well accepted by all, as he was imprisoned and executed in 399 BC. The efforts of Socrates and scholars after him were enlarged in the medieval period where dialogue was seen primarily in connection with a truth that was seen as a judge, and every discussion comes to an end through conflict resolution (Spranzi, 2011).

Just as Aristotle furthered the thoughts of Socrates, among the many scholars who amplified the thoughts of Aristotle on dialogue, according to Spranzi, were Carlo Sigonio, Sperone Speroni, and Torquato Tasso, who wrote various academic works on this subject in the second part of the sixteenth century (2011: 133). These authors view dialogue as having a connection with dialectic, disputation, and poetics. They claim it has much to do with the image of disputation as in a play, with protagonists and villains each playing his/her own part in an argument. Spranzi further argues that in the Renaissance, dialogue was "considered as a means of progressing towards the truth and as a means of evaluating opposite arguments and reaching probable conclusions" (2011:135). In the twentieth century, the efforts of David Bohm, William Isaacs, and a host of others have brought the dialogue discourse to a higher level.

It is often said that the most authentic photograph is the one taken without you noticing that you were about to be photographed. In that instance, you are just yourself. The moment the camera focuses on us, we tend to act up by adjusting a lot of things around us, and we cease to be original. Now, imagine what happens when you meet at a conference or gather for a meeting in the office. Before the conference or meeting commences, people gather in small groups to banter and share ideas, laugh over small jokes, and generally communicate in an open and non-judgmental way. As the meeting begins, people assume roles, with each one playing his or her part either as the boss or the staff, the guest speaker or the audience. What happens at this stage is the loss of the authenticity hitherto witnessed in the informal gathering. In the formal setting, thoughts are processed before anything is said and sometimes originality is lost.

After the meeting begins, people often do not have "'real" dialogue but, as in a movie, they only play a role in saying what others expect them to say. One of the key ingredients to having a fruitful dialogue is to avoid the temptation of having a fixed mind on ideas. Sometime we tend to come to the table with already made-up mindsets that give little or no room for considering a contrary opinion. One of the rules of thumb I learnt in my undergraduate years of studying philosophy comes from Heraclitus who said that the only constant thing in life is change and that since life is in a constant state of change, one cannot step into the same body of water twice. As such, since life itself is a process, the act of engaging in dialogue should be seen along the same line, where rigidity gives in to fluidity of thought.

One of the great feats of the present civilization is the invention of the Internet, which has affected all aspects of human life. Be it commerce, politics, transportation, or communication, no facet of life is spared this sweeping tide of technological innovation. With special reference to communication, I remember in the 1980s when the landline held sway as the main means of telephonic communication, and this medium was in the homes of a privileged few, at least in Nigeria. In the present dispensation, the telephone is not only mobile but can do virtually anything and everything. People transact business on the phone, do their banking through the same medium, and many mobile phones contain more pictures than some photo studios.

Although this development is laudable, it has also fostered communication gaps between people. Apart from the digital divide, which these electronics present in the dearth of access to this means of communication among many people due to financial, educational, and social status reasons, even for those who do have access to these means, a gap is created in the way the modern means are used to the detriment of face-to-face communication.

For instance, there are occasions when a family of four travels in the same car and no one communicates with the others. While one is busy driving, another is occupied with Facebook on the cell phone, the third may be on Instagram, and the fourth occupant of the same vehicle might be playing a video game. With the modern means of communication, a great chasm continues to be seen in the aspect of dialogue, which hitherto cemented relationships and brought people together. I will talk more on the issue of dialogue and the digital age in a later chapter of this book.

Dialogue from the Cultural Perspective

Culture is said to have an immense influence on the totality of the human person. Scholars view culture as the toolkit containing everything about the person (Swidler, 1986; Hays, 2000; Alexander, 2003; Milkie & Denny, 2014). Through culture, a people's way of life is preserved, modified, and transmitted in stories, songs, religious practices, and other socializing agents. Given that the human person is at the same time a cultural, social, and religious being, a lot can be learnt about the cultural dimension of dialogue from the major religions of the world. Most religions believe in the vital relationship between the adherents and a Supreme Being, a relationship that is fostered through a form of dialogue known as prayer.

In traditional African religion, adherents believe in the existence of a Supreme deity. Among the Yorubas of South West Nigeria, this Supreme Being is called Olodumare. He is said to be the Almighty, having no beginning and no end. He is said to be the one who created the world, but He has other smaller gods who assisted him in the act of creating humans and continue to help him maintain order in human society. One of these deities, Obatala, is believed among the Yorubas of Nigeria to have been given the task of molding the head of each individual in existence. The head is held in very high esteem among the Yorubas as it is said to determine one's destiny.

I remember as a young child, watching a television program that portrayed the relationship between Olodumare, the different gods, and one's head. For kids growing up in South-west Nigeria in the 1970s and 1980s, *Ifa-Olokun As'oro d'ayo* was a popular TV program that portrayed and educated viewers on issues around *Olodumare*. Ifa corpus is a body of wise sayings attributed to the god of divination. Ifa is said to be one of the gods, and it is seen as a cultural system containing "a veritable source and inspiration for the ethos, normative value, yearnings, fears, hopes, joy, and the whole system of thought with which the Yoruba race is identified" (Akintola, 1999:3).

The brain behind this program, Chief Yemi Elebuibon, is a traditional Ifa priest and therefore, the stories were not only touching but also educative and factual, according to the Ifa corpus. One of the Ifa corpuses depicted in a drama back then was about the importance of the human head (destiny) and the need to have daily dialogue (prayer) with one's head before embarking on anything in life. The Yorubas say, *"Ori ni ka bo, ka fi orisa sile"*. That is, "Sacrifices should be offered to one's head instead of being offered to the gods." In this saying, despite the high regard they have for the gods, the Yorubas hold that one's head has a key role to play in whatever happens to someone and the best way to avert evil is by having constant dialogue with one's destiny through sacrifices and prayers.

In the drama about the importance of *Ori* (head/destiny), the storyline depicts two friends, Orilonise and Tobalase, who lived beside each other and were both praise-singers to the king of their village. Those days, kings were so powerful and no day passed without praise-singers chanting at the top of their lungs about the king's prowess. There were, however, stark differences between the two friends in going about their profession. Orilonise begins his chant everyday by appeasing his Ori before chanting the king's praises. On the contrary, Tobalase goes straight into telling about the might of the king without any recourse to his Ori. The difference in the approach of these two individuals bothered the king. He wondered why Orilonise disrespected him by first appealing to his Ori instead of immediately chanting the king's praises. At that point, he decided to set a test for the two men to see who was right or wrong in their approach.

The king informed the two men that he had a special gift for them and that they should come the next day to get it. Since the two friends lived close to each other's house, instead of going at the time they usually resumed for duty, Tobalase sneaked out of the house in the wee hours of the morning in order to arrive at the palace before his friend. The king had earlier prepared two calabashes for the two men. He told Tobalase to pick the one of his choice. Tobalase looked keenly at the two and picked the one that appeared to be the biggest. He thanked the king and went home. Much later Orilonise arrived and had no choice but to pick the remaining calabash. He also thanked the king and went home. Since the two men lived beside each other, they both called their wives to the patio to unwrap the king's gifts.

Tobalase, who was the first to get to the palace to pick the big calabash opened it and was happy to see well-prepared pounded yam plus the local soup and bush meat, which was a delicacy among the people of that village. He felt happy with himself and called his family to join him in the feast. On the contrary, when Orilonise opened his calabash, he only found a small portion of pounded yam but no soup or meat to go with it. Tobalase looking from afar saw his friend's predicament and felt pleased with himself, thinking the king had rewarded him for going straight to praise him, instead of wasting time like his friend who always began by appealing to his Ori.

Orilonise's wife was also not happy with her husband, seeing how the couple in the next compound was enjoying pounded yam with a delicious soup, while they had nothing with which to eat the pounded yam. She mocked her husband and reminded him how earlier that day, she had told him to ensure he got to the palace in good time, but instead he used a greater part of the morning in dialogue with his Ori, all in the name of appeasement. Despite this chastisement from his wife, Orilonise admonished her to keep trusting in their destiny. He made her understand that his daily dialogue with his Ori was sure to lead him on the right path. He reminded her of the full meaning of his name, Orilonise Eda l'ayanmo, that is: "One's head makes the way to a person's destiny."

To this end, he asked his wife to bring water to drink with the king's pounded yam. It was not a delicious choice but the wife joined him to eat. As they struggled to eat their meal, all they heard were laughter and jeers from the other compound as Tobalase and his wife made fun of them. Orilonise and his wife, however, continued to "enjoy" the king's food. However, towards the end of the meal, as they were about to take the last two morsels of the food, something strange happened. They noticed something very strong in their hands, and when they rinsed the food away from this object, they saw a very precious stone hidden away in the food. Their joy knew no bounds as they discovered that Ori was truly appeased by the unceasing dialogue.

They noted that if Orilonise had not always engaged in that inner dialogue with his Ori before chanting the king's praises, the king might not have been moved to do any of this in the first place. Again, if he had not dialogued with his Ori that morning, but rushed to the palace before Tobalase, he might have been the one to pick the wrong calabash. When he sold the precious stone discovered in his food, he bought horses, land, and other luxuries that people valued in his time. This made the king believe further in Orilonise and his appeal to his Ori. This particular episode of the drama ended with the king giving an order that everyone in his kingdom should constantly have dialogue with their Ori through sacrifices and daily prayers.

Another episode of this program that featured the importance of dialogue was the story of two other friends, Ogbe and Owonrin. This is a part of the Ifa corpus that shows how dialogue fosters relationships and how a breakdown of the same can result in untold consequences. The play depicted Ogbe and Owonrin as very good friends. They never did anything without consulting each other. The communication model between the two was a thing of envy among other villagers.

In those days, farming was the main occupation among the locals, but for whatever reason, there was a serious drought in the land. Fields produced no harvest, leading to excruciating famine in the land. One fateful day, Ogbe went to the farm to see if the trap he set for wild game had made a catch so that he could have something to feed his family. To his surprise, even the wild game refused to take the bait. He was dejected, but while going back home something strange happened.

Ogbe saw an elderly lady who was trying to lift a load of firewood onto her head, as was the custom in those days. Ogbe stopped to assist the lady by carrying the load himself to the lady's destination. As a show of gratitude, the lady brought out a seed of cocoa and gave to Ogbe. She told him he should plant the seed and ensure it was well watered and protected so that it could grow. Ogbe was taken aback by this gift from the old lady. He wondered in his mind how a single seed could solve the huge problem of feeding himself and his family with the famine in place. However, he thanked the lady, collected the seed, and went home. Instead of going straight to his own home, he went to his friend Owanrin's house. He narrated all that had happened and how he was on the verge of throwing the seed away. He said he only came to inform his friend, since they both never did anything without first informing the other.

The friend told him to do as the old lady commanded. Ogbe wondered how he would protect the seed from goats and other domestic pets when it began to sprout. Looking around his friend's compound, he saw a clay pot with an open base. He told Owanrin that, if he was to obey the old lady, he would need the broken pot to protect the cocoa seed from being eaten by house pets. Owanrin gladly gave his friend the pot he requested. With trepidation but hope in the old woman's words, Ogbe went back home and planted the single cocoa seed. Normally it takes about 5 years for a cocoa tree to mature and produce first pods. However, like a miracle, the seed planted by Ogbe grew and started producing in five weeks.

Ogbe's single cocoa seed did not just grow into a very big tree, it also produced a bumper harvest like no one had ever witnessed in their village. Cocoa is an export crop with a very high monetary gain for anyone who engages in that trade. This catapulted Ogbe from his previous poverty-stricken social stratum to the caliber of the rich and influential in his village. He wielded so much influence, power, and prestige in the community that the king of their village awarded him a chieftaincy title in recognition of his wealth and support for the community.

While all this was going on, the communication between Ogbe and Owanrin dwindled, since the latter now became envious of his friend's newfound fortune. The duo, who had hitherto engaged in a form of dialogue that was a model for the whole community, now saw each other sparingly. Every effort made by Ogbe to draw his friend closer to him proved abortive. The break in communication between these two friends soon became the talk of the town.

Owanrin's envy of his friend's newfound wealth soon graduated to the level of enmity. He looked for a way to stop his friend's source of income, but found none. One day, in his moment of reflection, he remembered the bottomless pot he had given his friend when he wanted to plant the cocoa seed, and he decided to collect it back. He thought to himself that his pot was the foundation of Ogbe's riches, and once he got it back, it would mark the end of Ogbe's wealth.

As such, Owanrin went to the king of their village to lay a complaint against Ogbe with the sole aim of getting his pot back. The king sent for Ogbe and narrated the demand of Owanrin. Ogbe laughed it off, explaining to the king how his friend would not make such request. To Ogbe's surprise, Owanrin came into the palace at the same moment and said to his face that he needed his pot back. Ogbe reminded him of how close friends they used to be and that the pot was given many years ago. He implored the king to plead on his behalf; however, every intervention from the king fell on Owanrin's deaf ears.

The king asked the two friends to go home, dialogue together as they used to do, and come back to him in three days' time. On the third day, Owanrin was the first to arrive in the palace with the same request to have his pot back. When every effort at dialogue had failed, the king asked Ogbe to return his friend's pot. Ogbe said the only way to get the pot out of his cocoa tree would be to break it. Owanrin vehemently opposed this idea, saying he wanted his pot in the same manner it was given to Ogbe. Ogbe retorted that if the pot was not broken, he did not know any other way to get the pot out. Upon hearing this, Owanrin said the cocoa tree should be cut down so that his pot could be retrieved intact.

The people in the palace fell silent at Owanrin's demand since this entailed cutting down the tree that the entire village knew was the source of income for Ogbe and would render him and his family poor. Ogbe could not accept being taken back to his former state of abject poverty and, most importantly, on account of mere jealousy by someone he once considered as his friend. Everyone intensified the plea for Owanrin to let go of the pot, but he would not budge. Seeing the turn of events, the king commanded that Ogbe's cocoa tree be cut and the pot retrieved and given to Owanrin. The king's order was immediately carried out. Owanrin went home a happy man while Ogbe's sadness knew no bounds.

A few weeks after the ugly incident at the king's palace, Ogbe returned to the king. This time, he wanted something in return to demand of his former friend, Owanrin. When everything had been going well between the two of them, Owanrin's daughter had married and, in those days, to have a gold neck chain for your wedding was a sign of prestige and affluence. In preparation for the wedding, Owanrin had approached Ogbe to ask for assistance in getting a gold chain for his daughter. Ogbe had agreed to this request and paid the blacksmith to have the gold chain made.

In those days, neck chains did not have hooks as they do today enabling the wearer to easily put them on or take them off. Back then, the blacksmith mixed the raw gold and molded it around the neck of whoever wanted one. The gold chain could not be removed from someone's neck once it was fixed. Following the same pattern as when Owanrin had asked for his bottomless pot, Ogbe asked that the chain not be cut but taken from the lady's neck in whatever way possible. The only way to get it off, if the chain was not to be cut, would be to cut the neck on which it hung. This made Ogbe's request sound very ridiculous to Owanrin.

To this end, Owanrin simply laughed it off when he was told by the king of his friend's demand. When he saw how serious and adamant Ogbe was about his demand, however, he began to plead with the king, asking that he should be given some time to dialogue with his friend. Like in the other instance, the king again told the duo to go and talk it over, but Ogbe retorted that there was nothing to talk about. According to him, just as Owanrin had no room for dialogue before cutting the cocoa tree that was the source of livelihood for himself and his family, there would be no dialogue for the case at hand.

This episode of the drama ended in a dilemma as to what we, the audience, would have the king command Owanrin do at the end of the day. If the king were to give the same kind of verdict as he had given in the case of the pot and the cocoa tree, Owanrin's daughter would have to be beheaded in order to release the gold neck chain. This is why the Yorubas say: "Owanrin se Ogbe, Ogbe se Owanrin", that is, if Owanrin hurts Ogbe, Ogbe can as well hurt Owanrin. In this drama, we see the importance of dialogue and how a break in communication due to envy, jealousy, or any other factor can result in dire consequences for people.

Apart from the importance of the dialogue between the human person and his/her Ori, or in the story between Ogbe and Owanrin, the Ifa-Olokun television program also highlighted dialogue among the lesser gods. It is believed that this dialogue brings about oneness, since those who worship the god of iron (Ogun) join others who worship the river goddess (Osun) each time they celebrate their own deity, while the Sango worshippers also celebrate with the Obatala adherents. This collaboration, communication, and dialogue towards peace is still seen among adherents of traditional religions today.

One of the songs in the Ifa-Olokun TV program goes thus, *"E j'Onifa ko bo'fa, e j'Olosun ko b'Osun, e j'Oloro ko b'Oro, k'aye ko le gun."* That is, allow the adherents of the god of divination, the river goddess, and masquerade followers to worship their various gods for peace to reign in the world. While guarding against syncretism, which is the practice of worshipping more than one god, we can learn something from the unity among these traditional worshippers.

My point in presenting these stories is to show that in traditional religions, peace is the main goal and this peace is attained through dialogue and joint celebration in the affairs of one another. A vivid example is the Osun Osogbo festival, a celebration of the river goddess in Osun State of Nigeria, which gathers not just believers of other smaller gods but also international spectators each time this festival is held. This goddess is believed to be one who brings about fertility in women, and as such, the town of Osogbo is always agog each time the festival is celebrated. In the traditional religions of Nigeria, therefore, dialogue is an essential aspect of life and worship. Believers hold that the gods come from the same source, and dialogue among the gods and between them and Olodumare is what brought the world into existence as well as what keeps the world in being.

Having grown up in Ibadan in South-Western Nigeria, Africa, in the 1970s and 1980s, continues to give me some sense of nostalgia. This was the period before the advent of the present technological innovation of computers and other digital formats that connect people across the globe. Despite the lack of these luxuries, Africans are not only dialogical but also participatory in every facet of life. The rich proverbs and stories Africans tell elicit an engaging feedback. As young children growing up in 1980s Nigerian society, we looked forward to every evening when we would gather under a big tree in front of our house and elders in the community would take turns telling us stories that were not only rich in cultural heritage but also very high in moral teachings. At that time, there was no staying glued to computer screens, since, at any rate, there were none. The circular mode of sitting around an elder gave us the opportunity to communicate in such a way that everyone felt involved.

The form of communication in the storytelling was highly dialogical in the sense that most of the stories told included songs, which we sang at intervals as the narration progressed. Moreover, at the end of each story, the narrator asked us to tell him what moral we were able to decipher from the story. This was a way of discovering whether we were following the story and also to provide feedback on what we had heard. Anyone who gave a wrong answer to the questions asked at the end of the story would receive a good laugh from peers who would, at the same time, be raising their hands in an effort to be the one to answer correctly.

A good response to the questions asked would not only earn us the praise of the elder, but also the admiration of our peers. One might even be lucky enough to get a treat from the elder who narrated the story. As such, we listened intently, sang joyously, and we were always ready to give the appropriate feedback at the end of each story. The kind of dialogue that ensued in these moonlight tales engendered active participation in all of us, and lessons learnt in such gatherings continue to shape and guide us even as adults.

One of the many stories we were told as children, which was not only rich in cultural heritage and moral values but also brought out the ideal of sacrifice for a higher good, was the story of Moremi Ajasoro. Like many such stories, this particular story resonates with me due to the dialogical manner in which it was told. Moremi was a queen in Ile-Ife. Ile-Ife, which is believed to be the cradle of Yoruba civilization, used to be part of the old Oyo State but is currently a town in Osun State, South-Western Nigeria. In fact, oral tradition holds that it is from Ile-Ife that the day dawns for the entire world; hence, the saying: *"Ife ooye, ibi ojumo ti nmo w'aye."*

The story goes that many years ago, the people of Ile-Ife were attacked by barbarians, who raped their women, carted away their male folk, and plundered their land. The Bush Tribe invaders were a fierce-looking and dreadful group of people, and the Ife people dared not stand in their way due to their scary look and the belief that they were gods. This went on for years. Moremi was troubled to see her people subjugated under such heavy burdens of slavery, plunder and destruction at the whims and caprices of these barbarians.

In light of all that was happening, Moremi sought different ways to put an end to the oppression of her people, but to no avail.

Among others, she consulted the goddess of Esimiri River who promised to give her the solution to their predicament if she was ready to fulfill an oath the goddess would request of her after the resolution of her people's plight. Moremi promised to do whatever the goddess would demand of her. At this, the goddess told her to be prepared to be taken as a slave when next the invaders came and she gave her the charm needed to withstand the ordeal. It was while in captivity that she discovered the secret of the Bush tribe. She got to know they only camouflaged to deceive Ife people and that they only needed to be unmasked to reveal their true identity.

Moremi was taken aback by how simple the solution to the problem they had grappled with for many years sounded. When she returned home and told the villagers the solution to their plight, her suggestion was taken with a pinch of salt. The villagers wondered who will bell the cat? After many appeals, a few persons led by Moremi volunteered and prepared for the fateful day when the barbarians would march to their land in the hope of plundering and carting away the booty as usual. When they did, to their surprise, the people of Ile-Ife stood their ground and arrested and unmasked the aggressors. Thus, they discovered that the invaders were not gods as they hitherto had believed, but mere mortals camouflaged with palm fronds to scare the people away.

After being stripped of their disguise, the invaders were then chased away; those among them who were caught were enslaved by the Ife people. That was the end of the suffering they had endured for many years at the hands of the barbarians. The people were more than over-joyed at their deliverance through the instrumentality of the brave queen, Moremi. With victory won, Moremi went in haste to thank the Esimiri River goddess for helping to conquer the barbarians and to ask what the goddess would demand of her in fulfillment of the promise made. At this point, the goddess asked for Moremi's only child, Oluorogbo to be sacrificed! This did not go down well with Moremi, and she did everything to appease the goddess so that she would ask for something else. The goddess was adamant and reminded Moremi that her word should be her bond. The entire town gathered to appease the goddess, but to no avail.

At this point, the narrator told us how the Ile Ife people burst out in a mournful song: *Moremi Ajasoro, ewure O hun mi ma maa gba o*! As he sang that part, we all chorused the refrain – *Moremi Ajasoro*! The story concluded with Moremi having to fulfill her promise by giving up her only child in sacrifice for the salvation of her entire people. Some of these stories have happy endings while some others ended in tragedy, albeit, for a higher good. The narrator then asked us, sometimes tearful after hearing such stories filled with mixed feelings, what lesson we had deduced from the story. The dialogical part of the stories included the melodious music where there was back and forth between the narrator and us. Most importantly, dialogue comes to the fore in this meaning-making process at the end, as we rub minds together to hear what meaning each of us derived from the stories.

Apart from dialogic participation in moonlight tales, participation is generally an important part of life for the African. Within the traditional African family, joint participation and cooperation strengthens kinship ties. It is believed that, "*Bi nnkan ba kan enikan ninu ebi, ibaa je ebi ti a dijo ngbe agbo ile tabi eyi ti o ngbe agbo ile miran, gbogbo ebi naa lokan*" (Ladele, 1986:98; Babatunde, 1992:228). That is, if anything happens to anyone within the family, be it someone who lives in the same compound with his siblings or lives apart, it concerns everyone else in the extended family. When a child is born, experienced elderly wives take delivery and for the few weeks after giving birth, the biological mother may not have the infant except for breastfeeding, since the child is safe in the hands of co-wives and other members of the family. As the child grows, he or she is socialized into the community through the warmth, fellow feeling, and dialogue that cement kin ties.

In the Yoruba environment, the Yoruba person sees the interdependence of his/her life with others. The community does not force an unyielding individual; rather the individual, through socialization, love, and concern that the household and community extends to him or her cannot now see himself or herself as anything apart from the community (Gbadegesin, 1991:63). In this vein, Beller holds:

> The relationship between the individual and the community is of a functional-dialogic order. Symbolically, the individual assumes his or her function, which is to contribute to the life of the community or vital force which inserts itself into the material and spiritual cosmos. This function is not of a mechanistic type or only a moral obligation; it is decisively of the ontological order. As an individual he exercises his personal, social, and cosmic role linked to the faculties and tasks which are his own – as his gift – as a person to the community (2001:38-39).

Although, to a large extent, traditional African society is dialogical and participatory, as seen in my experience of growing up in the 1970s and 1980s Nigerian society, the same may not be said today. Like many other parts of the globe, the new wave of technological innovation of the 1990s has greatly affected the African continent. Urbanization, which came with the promise of transforming African communities and making them like big cities in North America and Europe, has brought some level of individualism which has adversely affected the hitherto dialogical nature of family ties.

Many places in Nigeria are becoming mega cities with a lot of traditional institutions giving way to Western comforts. This comfort, however, comes with adverse effects. For example, the Internet and cable television have replaced the get-together in many families. According to Nixon, "This new phenomenon, to ignore the real people we are with in favor of the digital people at the end of a wireless connection, is creating more implications than most people recognize. We have never been connected with as many people as we are today while at the same time being more isolated and unable to dialogue" (2012: 44). The new media and its effects on the dialogical aspect of life will be further treated in subsequent parts of this book.

In Canada, a great deal of effort in dialogue can be found among the Indigenous people of Canada and their relationship with nature. Living in this part of the world for many centuries, the First Nations, Inuit, and Metis developed ways of survival in the bitter cold winters before the advent of modern heating systems, through their connection and communication with nature. In more recent times, the effort at establishing dialogue between the Indigenous and modern Canadians is seen in the Truth and Reconciliation Commission, which was charged with the responsibility of fostering understanding between many facets of Canadian society and its Indigenous community, with special reference to the Indian Residential School system.

The Truth and Reconciliation Commission is a way of furthering the effort espoused in the Statement of Reconciliation of January 7, 1998. This concerns mostly the First Nations, Metis, Inuit, and families of former residential school students. Although some persons still doubt the extent to which this commission has been successful and the journey into effective dialogue seems slow and winding, suffice to note that with persistence, it leads to the safe harbor of understanding and true reconciliation. There is need to acknowledge the efforts of the Canadian government, among other nations of the world, who have to relate with their Indigenous populations.

The same issue of reconciliation through dialogue was experienced in South Africa at the end of apartheid and the beginning of that nation's emergence as a sovereign democracy. In his celebrated book, *Long Walk to Freedom,* Nelson Mandela narrated what the natives endured for many years in the hands of the colonial powers. The call, at the start of nation building in the 1990s, was thus for the nation to heal through dialogue, truth, and reconciliation. One sees a similar scenario in Nigeria upon the country's return to democratic rule in 1999, after many years of military dictatorship. The dialogue that forms a great part of this reconciliation effort seems to be blunt and to the point due to the many years of pain and suffering people endured.

Suffice to say, blunt and frank dialogue often brings about a situation where people find themselves on either side of the fence in defense of their action or as complainants. As such, it is pertinent to note that, "Due to the nature of truth commissions and despite the quality of their dialogue and the truth they surface, there are proponents and detractors" (Nixon, 2012: 307). Consequently, dialogue is replete with hurdles as people try to shift ground and meet another person at some mid-point of positions hitherto held. It is pertinent to note that no matter how difficult it may seem, some dialogues are inevitable not just for national development but also for peace in the minds of individuals.

Dialogue from the Christian Dimension

In the Christian tradition, the Bible began with the narration of God who engaged in dialogue at the very beginning of creation: "Come, let us make man in our own image" (Gen. 1:26-27). Some commentators of scripture believe that by the use of the words "let us", God was speaking to the other persons of the Holy Trinity, that is, Jesus Christ and the Holy Spirit. The Catholic Creed professes that Jesus Christ is co-eternal with the Father but only became manifest in human form in time to redeem humanity. This is confirmed in Jesus' saying that the Father and himself are one (Jn. 10:30). Again, the communitarian and dialogic attribute of God is further seen in the way the creation narrative explains how God would come to have conversations with Adam and Eve until the duo disobeyed a command God gave them and, through a process of dialogue, God gave them an opportunity to argue their case in the first form of tribunal in human history (Gen. 3: 8-15).

The Christian faith holds that throughout history, God had always longed to have a conversation with his people. He says through the Prophet Isaiah, "Come let us talk it over" (Is. 1:18). In the New Testament, Jesus exemplified the act of dialogue in the way he called his apostles and performed miracles by eliciting from people what they desired from him in a dialogical way (Mk 10:51). Worthy of note is the dialogue between Jesus and the woman at the Well of Jacob (Jn 4: 1-42). Through a gentle but enlightening dialogue, Jesus laid bare before the woman at the well her whole life history.

Starting from a request for water, Jesus made her understand that he would give her the water of life such that she would no longer be thirsty again. This dialogue between these two individuals later snowballed into what affected the entire community positively, since after having listened to Jesus, they later requested

Him to remain with them. This encounter between Jesus and the Samaritan woman will be further explored in a later part of this book.

Jesus' dialogical methods of teaching and personal examples were followed by Christians in the early Church. This is seen in the choice of Judas' replacement to complete the twelve apostles. It was not a decision taken by one person; rather, it was through a process of prayer, dialogue, and democratic way of the ballot that Matthias was chosen (Acts. 1:12-26). We, as well, see dialogue at play during the very first Council called by the early Christian community in Jerusalem. When dispute broke out as to what was needed for the Gentiles to become Christians, and some believed they had to be circumcised according to the Jewish custom while others held that baptism was all they needed, James presided over the Council. In a dialogical way, both sides of the argument were presented before a decision was taken (Acts 15: 12-21).

The dialogical method was employed by Peter in pronouncing Gentiles fit for the kingdom when, in a trance, he was made to understand, that with God, everyone is clean (Acts 10:1-20). Paul, one of the apostles of Jesus, albeit the least as he chose to call himself, engaged the dialogical method in presenting the Gospel message. A case in point happened in Athens. Paul was distressed by the level of idolatry in Athens, and when he began to reason with both the Jews and God-fearing Greeks in that city, they took him to the *Areopagus*, a place of meeting where they shared ideas and engaged in dialogue (Acts 17: 16-22). In this place, despite all obstacles he encountered, Paul presented his argument in the same dialogical manner the people were used to.

In the examples cited above, we see that, in tandem with the teachings of Christ, dialogue was an essential aspect of the early Church. It is little wonder that the Christian faith, in the present dispensation, keeps searching for better ways to foster dialogue among its various adherents in what has been termed inter-denomination dialogue. This is an effort of the World Council of Churches with members in more than 110 countries. While not imposing the doctrines of individual churches on one another, this body offers a space where Christians can support each other, pray, reflect, and work together. The WCC aims: "Not to build a global 'super-church', nor to standardize styles of worship, but rather to deepen the fellowship of Christian churches and communities so that they may see in one another authentic expressions of the 'one holy, catholic and apostolic church'" (Nixon, 2012: 293).

In the 5 years that I have been pastor of a cluster of three parishes in the Roman Catholic diocese of Saskatoon – Allan, Colonsay, and Viscount – the Christian community in Allan, which out of the three communities still has other churches apart from the Catholic Church, keeps engaging in dialogue among the three Christian Churches (Roman Catholic, Baptist, and United Church) there. Apart from gathering on a rotational basis in different churches for prayer during the yearly Week of Prayer for Christian Unity, we also get involved in the Fall Supper and other social activities of one another.

Following the dictates of Christ, her founder, the Roman Catholic Church has been committed to unity through dialogue from time immemorial. One of the ways the Catholic Church has done this in the twentieth century is through the Pontifical Council for Promoting Christian Unity, which was established as the Secretariat for Promoting Christian Unity on June 5, 1960 by then Pope John XXIII. Another broad step taken towards dialogue, not only between people of the Christian faith but also those of other religions, was on Pentecost Sunday, 1964, when Pope Paul VI instituted what was then called the Secretariat for Non-Christians, but has since been renamed in 1988 as the Pontifical Council for Inter-religious Dialogue by Pope St. John Paul II. At the inception of this body in 1964, Paul VI stated clearly that dialogue is a two-way communication that has to do with giving and receiving, speaking and listening in a way that enriches all involved parties.

This effort at dialogue by the Catholic Church is not limited to the Councils mentioned above, since, in many Church documents, dialogue comes to the fore as a way of promoting peace and unity in human society. In the 53rd World Day of Peace message, titled "Peace as a Journey of Hope: Dialogue, Reconciliation and Ecological Conversion", Pope Francis emphasized the importance of Peace in the context of our current society.

In that document, the pope narrated a few painful experiences that prevent peace for many persons on the global front and called for all in authority and everyone who desires peace to work for the peace of others. The pontiff affirmed the importance of dialogue in this effort at obtaining world peace. According to him: "We need to pursue a genuine fraternity based on our common origin from God and exercised in dialogue and mutual trust. The desire for peace lies deep within the human heart, and we should not resign ourselves to seeking anything less than this" (Francis, no. 1).

At various times, the present pontiff, Pope Francis, organized meetings for leaders of different world religions and political authorities in Assisi, Italy. Assisi, we must note, is identified with St. Francis, a saint known for care for nature and for peace. It is after this saint that the pope took his papal name, Francis, since he was known hitherto as Jorge Mario Bergoglio. The prayer of St. Francis for peace continues to be a formidable tool in dialogue towards reconciliation in many parts of the world: "Lord, make me an instrument of your peace; where there is hatred, let me sow love; where there is injury, pardon; where there is discord, union; where there is doubt, faith; where there is despair, hope; where there is darkness, light; and where there is sadness, joy."

The efforts of Pope Francis in working for world peace through dialogue is not limited to mere words but is also backed by concrete actions. How can anyone forget in a hurry the humble gesture of the Vicar of Christ and Bishop of Rome, when on April 11, 2019, Pope Francis knelt down to kiss the feet of South Sudan political leaders whom he had invited to the Vatican in a bid to find solutions to the political upheaval and imbroglio in their country. The shocked and embarrassed look on the faces of these politicians is priceless. This is not surprising since this follows the example of Jesus, who washed the feet of his disciples and told them to do likewise (Jn. 13:1-17).

The effort of the Church at promoting peaceful coexistence through dialogue is also seen in Pope Francis' latest encyclical letter, *Fratelli Tutti*, which was signed on October 3, 2020 in Assisi, on the vigil of the feast of St. Francis of Assisi. In the sixth chapter of this encyclical the pontiff holds that: "Approaching, speaking, listening, looking at, coming to know and understand one another, and to form common ground; all these things are summed up in the one word 'dialogue'" (no. 198).

While acknowledging many forces against dialogue in the present human civilization, Francis elaborates that it is through persistent and courageous dialogue that we can live better in the world. He points to the media of communication as that which can "help us to feel closer to one another, creating a sense of the unity of the human family which in turn can inspire solidarity and serious efforts to ensure a more dignified life for all" (no. 205).

Again, the impact of the Holy See is felt on the global stage as the Vatican sends delegates to the United Nations General Assembly and the United Nations Security Council and is also a permanent member of the United Nations Economic and Social Council. With more than 1.2 billion members all over the world, the presence of the Catholic Church in matters of dialogue is not limited to documents from the popes or efforts at the United Nations but most importantly, in many parishes and homes of the faithful across the globe. Through this presence on the world stage, the Holy See is able to influence policies aimed at peaceful and better world order. The aforementioned encyclical letter of Pope Francis, *Fratelli Tutti*, lends credence to this as it concludes by mentioning certain world leaders who promoted peace like Martin Luther King, Desmond Tutu, Mahatma Gandhi, and Blessed Charles de Foucauld and inviting all to emulate their example in our effort towards a more peaceful world.

Dialogue and Inter-religious Experience in Nigeria

It is pertinent to note, while not negating the efforts mentioned above, that dialogue continues to be hard to achieve even in Christendom today as some Churches do not have positive attitudes about Christians of other denominations. This appears to be more rampant in developing nations of the world. In Nigeria, for example, there are situations in which a big building complex of about three stories has each floor occupied by a different Church denomination.

In this situation, every Sunday becomes an occasion to see who can heap the most insults on those worshipping on a different floor of the same complex. They do this with very loud public address systems and with the preacher shouting at the top of his or her voice. What began in the place of worship is often extended to parking lots, as people of differing denominations use the same lot to park their vehicles, and getting in or out becomes a test in driving patience.

What occurs among the Christian denominations is like child's play compared to the difficulty at dialogue between Christians and

Muslims in many parts of the world. Despite the fact that these two religions both trace their roots to Abraham, inter-religious conflict between Christians and Muslims has been one of the main sources of death, carnage, and destruction in many African nations and around the world. People have assigned many reasons to this which go beyond the scope of this present book.

Suffice, however, to note that Pope Francis, in the declaration jointly signed with the Grand Imam of Al-Azhar, Ahmad Al-Tayyed, in Abu Dhabi, on February 4, 2019 highlighted some of the main reasons behind these conflicts as religious extremism, political crises, situations of injustice, and lack of equitable distribution of natural resources. Among others, they affirm that dialogue, understanding, and widespread promotion of a culture of tolerance, acceptance of others, and of living together peacefully would contribute to reducing the problems confronting humanity.

As someone who grew up in Nigeria, where Islamic fundamentalism has been a major bane, I would like to address the issue of dialogue from that personal experience. The rise of Islamic fundamentalism continues to defy any effort at dialogue, and the world stares in horror as people caught up in the crossfire cry daily for peace and an end to the carnage. We must note that Islam, like many other world religions, claims to be a religion of peace.

It would not be out of place to say that there are many peace-loving Muslims around the globe, but in a situation where some persons use the same religion to wreak havoc on believers of other faiths, it would not be out of place for those peace-loving individuals to call such elements who profess the same faith as themselves to order. The silence of many just persons is, in some way, giving a free hand to the destruction caused by a few.

In Nigeria, a nation of about 200 million people, where people were brought up with the African ideal of fellow feeling and life is always celebrated, the story has not only been gory but also devastating in the last two decades, with untold loss of lives and destruction of properties. Growing up and attending elementary school in the late 1970s and early 1980s in Nigeria, life was good to say the least. As young pupils, prayers were said daily, both in the Christian and Islamic faith traditions on the Assembly ground before we filed into our various classrooms.

What occurred in the schools was also seen in neighborhoods, as the dichotomy between Christians and Muslims was not allowed to foster hate, since everyone celebrated with the other during religious festivities. I had Muslim friends with whom we could not wait for their Sallah meat to be ready so we could get a bite. To our young taste buds, there was something special about the ram slaughtered and cooked during Sallah. The same is true of my Muslim friends who waited eagerly for Christmas for the special chicken and jollof rice delicacy. Life was indeed good.

Although some individuals claim the seed of Islamic fundamentalism in Nigeria can be traced to 1960s when, as a nascent independent nation, Nigeria was charting the path for nationhood, fundamentalism became more entrenched in 1978 when the Constitutional Conference was convoked. Here, Northern Nigerian Muslims came with the idea of introducing civil Sharia law into the Federal constitution, and when this was not initially agreed to, they walked out of the National Conference. Sharia law was later allowed to stand, since it was seen as mere civil law that pertains to the Northern section of the country as their customary law. Shortly after that came the Maitatsine riot in Kano, which was quickly crushed, though many lives had already been lost.

Then came the military junta of General Ibrahim Badamosi Babangida, who was Nigeria's military Head of State from 1985 to 1993. Under Babangida's rule, Nigeria was made to join the Organization of Islamic Cooperation (OIC). When Babangida annulled the acclaimed free and fair June 12, 1993 general elections, which were said to have been won by Chief MKO Abiola, Ernest Shonekan was made Head of Interim Government, only to be sent packing by General Sanni Abacha months later.

During the military junta of Sanni Abacha in the 1990s, many Nigerians, especially young professionals, went to Sudan, became students under hardened Islamic fundamentalists, and returned with the sole aim of Islamizing Nigeria. It was during the Presidency of Olusegun Obasanjo, who was democratically elected President in 1999 after many years of military rule, that the seed, which had been sown in the late 1970s, arrived at its peak in Islamic fundamentalism.

About this time, a certain governor in one of the Nigerian Northern States introduced criminal Sharia law, taking this a notch above the civil Sharia law that had been put into the national constitution in 1978. The act of this governor emboldened *Jama'at Ahl as-Sunnah Lid-Da'wah wa'l-Jihad*, popularly called Boko Haram, which is the vernacular of the Arabic name, which means: "Western education is a taboo". This group was founded in 2002 by Mohammed Yusuf, who was believed to have been killed under questionable circumstances by security operatives.

After the demise of its leader, the Boko Haram group has, since 2010, unleashed untold mayhem on the young and old in Nigeria. Although their attacks are geared mainly towards Christians, some moderate Muslims have also become victims at their hands. In light of the destruction perpetrated by this group, churches have been burnt, schools raided, public markets bombed, and even military bases have been attacked.

The activities of Boko Haram got international attention when on April 14, 2014, the group kidnapped.276 young female secondary school girls (Chibok Girls), who were preparing for their final examinations in Chibok, a town in Borno State, North Eastern Nigeria. Up till the time of writing this book, many of the girls and others from different parts of Northern Nigeria, are still in the camp of the terrorists. Boko Haram has recently metamorphosed into what is called "Islamic State in West Africa" (ISWA). As in the case of other terrorist groups like Al Qaeda, ISIL, etc., Boko Haram and other splinter groups have turned a deaf ear to any form of dialogue towards resolving whatever might be their grievance.

Another clog in the process of dialogue between the Nigerian government and this group can be seen when, in the wee hours of February 19, 2018, they stormed the Government Girls' Science and Technology College in Dapchi, Yobe State, Nigeria and carted away about 110 young school girls. Many of their victims have been released, apart from Leah Sharibu, a young Christian girl who was said to have refused to be converted to Islam. Despite concerted efforts by the Nigerian and Chadian military and pleas from many non-governmental organizations, Leah is yet to be released.

On December 11, 2020, hundreds of secondary school students were again abducted when their school at Kankara in Katsina State, Nigeria was invaded by these criminals. The boys were released a week after their abduction without any of the perpetrators of this evil act being arrested. Many persons question how the boys were carted away through many villages without intervention by security operatives in the first place and how their release was accomplished. Activities of these terror groups are still ongoing while dialogue seems not to have been given a chance in resolving the ugly crisis.

Instances of Challenges to Dialogue in Relationships

Dialogue, which serves the good interest of not just individuals but also of families and nations, can be hampered in many ways. One of the main hurdles to dialogue is a situation whereby one party is ready and willing to dialogue while the other party sees no need for dialogue. How then, do you dialogue with someone who is not disposed to dialogue with you? This was the experience of Mike, a young man of African descent who presently resides in North America and is a self-proclaimed dialogue-doubter. In the course of writing this book, I came across Mike and, in a bid to comprehend his lack of belief in dialogue, we had a very lengthy discussion. With teary eyes, Mike looked at me and said he was not always like this, but life experience has taught him that there is little or nothing that can be achieved through dialogue.

Mike grew up in a strong faith-based African family where love of God and of others was paramount. He met Mary who came from a similar background, and they courted for a while. They had been married for almost ten years when Mike was transferred from work in his native African country to North America. Mike said, without sounding grandiose, that even before their marriage, he was everything to Mary whom he reminded over and over again that she was also an integral part of him, and as such, he could not imagine life without her.

According to Mike, Mary also displayed the same disposition towards him. In many instances, when Mary thanked him for anything he did for her, he quickly reminded her that she was his other half and that anything he did for her, he did for himself; as such, there was no need to thank him. Mary reciprocated Mike's kindness with the same level of affection, as she carried Mike along in her day-to-day activities and would not do anything without sharing it with Mike.

For the duo, it was a love made in heaven, and they were the envy of their friends and associates. When Mike met Mary, she was fragile, sickly, and often in hospitals on a regular basis. Despite contrary admonition from many quarters, Mike stuck with Mary and supported her through each health crisis. His support for

Mary was not just on health grounds, but he also guided and financially supported her educational pursuit to the level of obtaining a Master's degree. Apart from supporting her academically, most things Mary did for the first time in her adult life she did through the help of Mike. When Mary finished her post-graduate program and got a job in a rural community, Mike, who was then living in a big city, made Mary's workplace his second home. He visited often and supported whatever assignment she was given to ensure she succeeded in her work.

Then came a time when Mary had problems in her workplace. Mike did all he could to assist her to navigate the storm and ensured that she was not fired. They burnt the midnight candle together, brainstorming on the best way forward, and how best to present the matter to her superiors. Mike's support for Mary was not limited to her alone, but also extended to her family whom he took as his own family.

As is customary to African culture, Mary had been well known to Mike's family even before their marriage, and every member of Mike's family was very fond of her. Mike recounts that Mary was every man's dream of a wife. Being a combination of beauty and brains, she displayed a high sense of responsibility and was very supportive of Mike. As such, they shared virtually everything in common, including dreams of a lifetime together.

In all the years they were together, communication was a given fact. In moments when they had to be away from each other physically, they communicated by the telephone to check on one another almost every minute of the day. They made video calls to begin and end each day, just to be sure the other was doing okay. Shortly before Mike got transferred out of the country, Mary also got transferred from the rural community where she worked to a big city. At the initial stage of planning for his trip, Mike called Mary and explained everything about the journey to her and how they both needed to understand that this was for their good in the long run.

Mike said he made it clear to Mary that if, for any reason, she wanted him to stay back, he would do so and reject the transfer abroad. Mary expressed joy and made profuse promises that she would always be there for Mike and that nothing could ever come between them. She made several music videos detailing all the troubles she endured due to ill health, projects at school, and challenges in her workplace and how Mike stood by her all the way. She sent this video to Mike assuring him that, with all these, Mike should rest assured that all was well with them and the distance was nothing after all they had been through together.

On the day of Mike's travel, since Mary could not accompany him to the airport due to the nature of her work, she stood at the bus station where Mike was to board the bus to the airport, and with teary eyes said to Mike, "No matter how long it takes, I promise to be here waiting for you." Mike said those words of Mary's promise were like a shield around him as he arrived in North America to begin a life of loneliness, extreme cold weather, and isolation from home.

Mike said each time he felt depressed about being in a foreign land, away from family and friends, those words of Mary spurred him on. Within the year after Mike got to his posting abroad, he began the process of helping Mary to get a visitor's visa so she could come and spend some time with him and use the opportunity to access better medical care for her health challenges. For this, he had to take a loan from work to help Mary get all the necessary documents for her appointment at the embassy.

Unfortunately, Mary's visa to the North American country where Mike resides was not granted because she did not have a travel history. Both Mike and Mary felt sad at this turn of events; however, Mike was unrelenting in his effort to get Mary abroad.

He made another plan right away to get her to Europe, with the hope that after going to Europe, her next attempt at getting a visa to North America would be favorably considered. He went beyond only helping her with the visa and arranged accommodation plus finances for her European trip. Mike said he was not able to afford all these expenses and had to take loans for the sole purpose of giving Mary a treat, but he continued to tell her that everything he did for her, he did for himself.

It was while Mary was in Europe that she called Mike one fateful evening to say she was "feeling dry" towards him. Mike was taken aback and didn't understand what Mary meant by "feeling dry". He asked for clarification and all Mary said in return was that she had said all she had to say, that Mike had not done anything wrong, but she just needed some time to think things over! On hearing this, Mike felt his whole world crumble beneath him.

In the weeks and months that followed, he was in shock, he lost concentration at work, his health condition was greatly affected as he visited the hospital many times for various medical procedures, and he became depressed. It took the intervention of his family and friends to navigate through months of nightmare. Both his family and Mary's waded into the matter, but Mary was adamant in having nothing to say. Mike narrated that each time anyone asked what the matter was, all Mary said was: "I've said all I have to say or do you want me to lie?"

At the initial stage of this disturbing revelation by Mary, Mike was still hopeful and did all he could to connect and reason with the "love of his life". At the initial stage, each time he called, Mary would pick up his call and tell him she was busy with some people, no matter the time of day or night that Mike called. Despite this treatment, Mike was persistent, hoping against hope that maybe she needed time to process whatever she was going through and that things would soon take a better turn. After two years of checking on Mary and getting snubbed, Mike said Mary later began to ignore his chats and refused to pick up his calls. Mike said he explored all options so as to fix his relationship with Mary through dialogue, but she would have none of that.

At the end of his narration, Mike looked me straight in the eye and said: "This is a lady for whom I had lost many opportunities in a bid to make her happy. I took up the job abroad for the betterment of us both and our families. The promises she made to me kept me going before she changed. Apparently, when she got a job in the big city and with my absence, other things began to happen, and your guess is as good as mine. How do you dialogue with someone who is not ready to even listen to you?"

Mike said what has been a great pain to him, apart from the initial shock and ongoing incredulity in Mary's betrayal of his love and trust, was her total blockage of any effort towards dialogue. Mike said he understands that distance causes breakage in many marriages, but he was surprised at Mary's unwillingness to even speak with him. Since his ordeal began, Mike traveled to their home country thrice with the hope of having a conversation with his dear wife, but was rebuffed at all instances.

During the first visit, although it was not time for his annual vacation from work, he wanted to make the trip so as to nip the situation in the bud. As such, he obtained special permission, got a very exorbitant flight ticket due to the short period of time to plan for the trip, and headed for Africa. When he saw Mary and inquired what the matter was about and how they could fix things, she nonchalantly repeated what she had earlier told him: "I've said all I have to say, and there is nothing more to say." Nothing Mike said elicited any concrete reason from Mary.

Mike went back to his job after that visit a wounded but determined man to make things right with Mary. To his surprise, at his second visit a year later, Mary blatantly refused to even speak with him. He said he could not even describe the very sad experience he had on his third voyage to Africa. Due to these experiences, he began to question the efficacy of dialogue in fixing problems. There are many others who can identify with Mike's story, as their love life may have taken the same sad route.

What has been said of Mike and Mary above presents a glimpse into what happens, albeit on a larger scale, among some nations of the world. In situations where world leaders refuse to dialogue with one another to resolve differences, the end results are wars and unrest in many parts of the globe. It is often said that no war is ever won on the battlefield but at a round table when people decide to come together to dialogue, no matter what their differences may be.

It is, however, sad to note that not many nations consider the option of dialogue but head straight for the battlefield and prefer to remain on that field of war. Although there are many instances of inter-tribal wars, due to a breakdown in dialogue, even within the same nation (such as Hutus and Tutsis in Rwanda and Ife and Modakeke in Nigeria), a case in view for the purpose of this book is the relationship between the United States and the Islamic Republic of Iran.

A break in dialogue between these two nations started in the 1950s when a democratically elected Iranian President was removed from office, as some have claimed, through the intervention of the United States. This has skyrocketed over the years into wars, acts of terrorism, and loss of lives on both sides. The most recent expression of this deteriorated dialogue between these nations began in 2017, when President Trump opted out of the Iranian deal engineered by his predecessor, President Barack Obama, in conjunction with European allies, Russia, and China. This brought about renewed hostilities, which led to the killing of an Iranian General Qassem Soleimani on the orders of President

Trump on January 3, 2020. This act has generated lots of argument around the globe in favor of or against this killing.

In the wake of protests at the American embassy in Iraq in the first week of 2020, President Trump said he had intelligence reports that Soleimani was planning attacks on American interests in the region, and the best thing was to take him out. Some have questioned the veracity of this claim, citing the lack of any available facts to back it up.

Although Iran retaliated by firing rockets into the American military base in Iraq from where the missile that killed Soleimani was said to have been launched, the world woke to a rude shock when, on January 8, 2020, just five days after the death of the General, an Iranian surface-to-air missile brought down a Ukrainian civilian jetliner, flight number 752, killing all 176 passengers and crew on board.

Most of the passengers on this ill-fated flight were Iranian citizens, however, a great percentage of them were Canadians, while some others were Ukrainians, British, and other nationalities. In view of this, the United States' House of Representatives voted on a bill to limit the powers of the American President to take out perceived enemies. In their view, the power to declare war resides in the US Congress, after careful consideration of all options. The argument was that there are many bad persons in the world and, if the American President begins to unilaterally take out each one, in what kind of world are we going to be living?

As can be seen in this case, the United States House of Representative members were trying to emphasize the importance of dialogue, since breakdown in dialogue does not bring any good to either side of the divide. The Iranian-American case is just one of the many instances of international muscle-flexing leading to destruction and loss of lives, which could have been resolved if nations were ready to dialogue with one another.

Based on the story of Mike and Mary narrated above, and that between the United States and Iran, the fact remains that what occurs between individuals can also be found between nations. Even within the same family, dialogue is much needed among members. Unfortunately, intergenerational difference has been another major bane to dialogue. While many look to this mainly in the home front, suffice to say, it pervades every aspect of human interaction – be it in the family, workplace, or even religious institutions. I recently engaged in a conversation with a middle-aged Canadian gentleman who works as an engineer in a firm. He lamented how younger engineers rely heavily on modern gadgets to find out something as small as the distance between two close points.

According to him, many of his younger colleagues wondered how he was able to gauge the diameter of a piece of iron or a plank by simply looking at it. This engineer lamented how the dexterity with which they had worked before the innovation of modern gadgets has eroded in younger generations, who regard the older members of staff as dinosaurs, outdated and archaic. With this view about their senior colleagues, the young ones are not ready to engage in dialogue that could improve productivity. Rather, unhealthy rivalry is now the new order. The camaraderie that should be the hallmark of any workplace is thrown out when the younger ones have little or no regard for their senior colleagues. Surely, much can be learnt in college, but a great deal is also achieved through experience on the job.

This is the experience of a grandparent I had a conversation with recently. The gentleman complained that his grandchild claims to know everything and would not even engage him in any conversation. Hitherto, the young found solace in their grandparents and were willing to relay to them life issues that they would not even discuss with their parents. As such, they were able to drink from the well of knowledge, which only life experience gives with advancement in age. There was a television commercial I watched recently where the father was advising his first-time driver son on the need to be careful on the road, but the son would have nothing to do with what the father was saying. The son claimed to know it all. In a gentle but firm way, the father simply told him, "I know you do, but can we at least have this conversation?" Many young people do not listen until they cannot listen again.

The same is true of a movie I saw recently titled, *Sons of The Caliphate*. In it, a young lady was betrothed to the king of their town. The lady was, however, in the fast lane of life as she spent a great deal of her day on drugs and the night clubbing. She hid this side of her life from her parents and always portrayed a very religious girl in their presence. One day, her mother caught her doing drugs in her room. The mother was dumfounded and could not believe what she was seeing. She asked the girl how, why, and for how long this had been going on for despite all the opportunities she had to discuss it with her mother. The girl decided to take it out on the mother and told her to let her be. She said it was her life and she should be allowed to live it as she so desires. The anger of the mother knew no bounds.

The mother sat her down and reminded her that, no, this was not just about her or her dad or her mother. She said it was about her ancestors, her yet unborn children, and her entire generation. The mother told her that if she ruins her life doing drugs, everyone will be involved and she could not then say to them, "It is my life." Many parents have encountered attitudes similar to that of this young lady. The young claim to know it all or say that they need to live their life as they wish. For many of them, nothing is true unless it can be found online. A great deal of family time has been taken up by a fixation on tablets, phone screens, or musical gadgets. This lacuna in dialogue breeds a communication gap with its adverse effects both in the workplace and in the family.

In the religious sector, many Churches are witnessing a decline in attendance among the younger generation due to the inability of some young persons to engage with religious tenets. Many young families feel they know and have so much that God has no place in their lives. The resultant effect of this is an over-empha-sized human intelligence and a society on a fast race towards the precipice of self-annihilation. Therefore, this chapter explores dialogue not only in concept but also in practice. I have looked at the socio-cultural, religious, and practical aspects of dialogue. Through these different dimensions, the importance of dialogue in every aspect of human life was underscored. The next chapter explores the theoretical orientation that guided this book.

CHAPTER TWO

———•———

Dialogue through the Prism of Systems Theory

For the last five years, I have resided in Saskatchewan in Western Canada. Being one of the Prairie Provinces, Saskatchewan is fondly called the breadbasket of the world and the wheat province. With its very beautiful flat landscape and excellent view of sunrise and sunset, this province is also called the Land of the Living Skies. The province has 40% arable landmass, producing grains and oil-seeds. Saskatchewan is also known for extreme cold weather and has the world's largest deposit of potash and uranium.

Living in the prairies these years has further broadened my view on how the people of the province are connected to one another. It took me a while to realize that most persons in my cluster of parishes are cousins, distant relations, or brothers and sisters to one another. Here, every family seems to be related to the next. Hence, my stay in the prairie has further enlightened me on how humanity is intricately connected to one another and to nature.

Pope Francis had earlier made this connection in his Magna Carta, *Laudato Si*. In this encyclical letter on the Care for our Common Home, the pontiff called humanity to a renewed appreciation of the connection between humanity and nature. The pope began this encyclical by quoting Saint Francis of Assisi, who sang God's praises for the gift of nature which sustains and nourishes us, and which he referred to as "Our Sister, Mother Earth".

In number 14 of this encyclical, the Holy Father, Pope Francis, highlighted the importance of dialogue when he called for "a new dialogue about how we are shaping the future of our planet". For Francis, a renewed connection between the human person and the environment through authentic dialogue with one another and with nature cannot be over-emphasized.

In the same vein, in Saskatchewan, with only 4 months available in the year for farming, due to the extreme cold weather, people in the prairies have developed a close connection with "Mother Earth". This special connection enables them to know the right time to prepare the soil, plant the seeds, and harvest the crops before the cold winter sets in when the land freezes and the grains lose value if not harvested in good time. One of the highlights of my stay in Saskatchewan was my first time driving a combine.

A combine is a huge equipment with which farmers harvest their crops after swathing, which puts the cut stems on a straight stretch for easy gathering. The combine is a complex system, which does many things at the same time. All parts of this complex machine work together for efficiency and effective harvest. The combine picks up the stock of the crop that has been swathed from the ground, separates the grain from the chaff, puts the grain in the bin, shreds the stock, blows the shredded stock out onto the soil and, when the bin is full, offloads it into a waiting truck for onward transportation into a bigger bin.

When I climbed onto this gigantic machine the very first day, I was faced with a number of buttons/switches and wondered, where do I go from here? My friend who had invited me to his farm was a great help, as he showed me the right switches to press, not only to drive the combine, but also to pick up the crops and so on. For me, it was a great accomplishment to drive the combine along the rows of swathed crops and dump the final products into the moving semi-truck for onward transportation to the larger bins/barns. It is from the bins that farmers transport the crops to various grain terminals for sale.

After this, my first day on the combine, I was invited at various times later to help in harvesting wheat, peas, canola, etc. The example of the combine with its various functions in a single system shows how the human person is also a complex system, with each part of the system needed for effective functioning of the whole body. This is also true of persons in the communication process. Each participant is an important part of the whole system; for the system to be effective, each must function appropriately.

Recall what you experienced when you were taught to ride a bike. It must have seemed like a very complex feat to accomplish. You were made to understand that one foot pushes a pedal down while the other foot does the same at the next turn. If you push one foot on the pedal but fail to quickly press the second foot, you are apt to fall. To be effective in riding a bike, both legs must function simultaneously. What seemed so complex initially may begin to look simple later, but those basics of how to pedal were vital to the initial days of riding a bike. Even if you fall in your first attempts, those initial instructions help you subsequently.

In the field of social sciences, theories not only serve as the guides directing thought processes, but also they serve as the shoulders of giants upon which we stand to see more clearly into the horizon. A good theoretical background shows the relationship of prediction and how a piece of work proceeds. It also reveals whether the researcher has been faithful to the academic discipline of what he or she had set out to accomplish at the onset. Like the analogy of learning to ride a bike cited above, the theory is the step-by-step analysis that guides the study along a certain path until the final destination of how to best explain a scientific phenomenon is attained.

While some persons have trepidation at the thought of engaging in academic discourse in the form of building from a theoretical base, the example of my combine driving and that of riding a bike above should alleviate this fear, as theory is part of everyday human life, even when we do not notice it. We are all guided by certain rules and the theoretical foundation offers the privileged standpoint from which to proceed in any academic pursuit.

Albert Einstein was quoted to have said, "If I am able to see far into the horizon, it is because I am standing on the shoulders of giants." Theorists are those giants upon whose shoulders we stand to make projections, which are called hypotheses in academic circles. This is nothing else but a relationship of causation leading to prediction of events. For the purpose of this book, Systems Theory will be our guide.

Systems Theory was developed using the perspective of how elements of a system work together to produce outputs from the various inputs they are given. Defining a system, a proponent of this theory, Bertalanffy, says it is a "set of elements standing in interrelation among themselves and with the environment" (1975: 159). Bertalanffy, a German biologist, decried the way he believed science explained reality by dissecting it into various parts and treating each part as an entity, distinct from the whole. He referred to this as Scientific Reductionism.

For Bertalanffy, as elaborated by Connors (2011), everything is connected to the other in nature and that explains why levels of systems are said to be contained within the larger systems, from cells to organs, individuals, relationships, communities, states, the planet, and the universe. He used the example of the human body, which takes in food and passes out waste products, to explain what he calls an open system. For a system to endure, it must be open, having the capacity to take in and let out. No system can survive if it is closed in on itself. Thus, he saw the interconnectedness of everything in nature through the give and take that embodies all.

Connecting Systems Theory to interpersonal communication, Connors (2011) sees it in the form of a blood vessel and that what individuals in communication do is to feed off and contribute back into the system. Even when such relationships experience tensions and stress, the energy that each member brings on board helps to create a form of readjustment. Adam Heil's paper on General Systems Theory (January 2020) buttresses the thoughts of Bertalanffy and copiously elaborates those of Connors. Heil emphasizes the idea of readjustment earlier mentioned and calls it "homeostasis" – a way the system maintains equilibrium through feedback from its component parts. Consequently, communication, examined through the prism of System Theory, is never static but in constant flow through feedback which is exchanged at various stages of the communication process.

When communicating, persons dialogue and share ideas. What emerges is a synergy of individual ideas and thoughts, which is greater than what each person brings into the communication process. According to Systems Theory and in tandem with the true meaning of communication, dialogue is an open and ongoing process. This is because, as people dialogue with one another, they develop rules and patterns of conduct. This is what maintains equilibrium in the system without which each member may tend to see things only from his/her personal perspective and thus create problems for the process.

In this light, Heil (2020) holds that: "Problems are a sign of a malfunctioning process. When a system fails, it is because either a feedback channel is not working or the adaptation cycle is being ignored; both of these are functions of communication." Many relationships are malfunctioning today simply because communicating persons refuse to give the appropriate feedback at the right time!

Segrin and Flora applied Systems Theory to understanding communication within the family (the basis of human relationships), and they present certain processes to buttress this application. According to the duo, these processes are mutual influence, stability, change, feedback and calibration, and equifinality (2005: 30-32). By the first process, mutual influence, they hold that all family components are interdependent, in that what happens to one affects all. This is similar to what occurs in the African setting, as exemplified in the story of Moremi Ajasoro, where human life is held in communal affiliation. This mutual responsibility goes throughout the life of persons and at times parent-child roles, for example, may be reversed.

Even in Western countries, this reversal of roles is seen in the case where parents take care of their children by providing all their needs, and the children grow up to later take care of the parents in their old age. It is interesting how parents take their children to the doctor, for movie nights, restaurants, etc., and when children grow up, they do the same for their parents. The sight of parents in their senior years being taken to the beach by their children is priceless. This first phase of the process leads to the second, which they refer to as stability. Stability has some level of predictability, which is seen as I have explained in the practice of parents caring for their wards and the children doing the same at a later stage for their parents.

Just as stability is essential to the family, Segrin and Flora hold that change is also needed. The change they talk about is to be seen in the fact that families are not static but evolve over time. As people inter-marry from different cultures, children are born who must relate with the various cultural backgrounds that define them. Not only do families change, but also the way people look at those who constitute the family. There were times in the past when people claimed, and erroneously so, that "the woman's place was in the kitchen". Present day reality has proven otherwise.

The globalization drive of the present society has done a lot to bring changes to family life and to the means of communication. This leads to Segrin and Flora's fourth process in the explanation of Systems Theory: feedback and calibration. This is because in the present global village, information seems to move faster than the speed of light and family members and those engaged in any communication process become information processors as they examine their way of life and compare it with others around them.

The final process as explained by Segrin and Flora is known as "equifinality" and this states that the same end can be achieved using different means. For example, in some families, all members work to "make ends meet". In others, only the father and mother work or it is only the father who works outside the home. The main thing is to make ends meet for the individual families.

What has been said of the family here connects also with the different roles each communicating party plays in the whole process of meaning making. The roles are reversed when one is the originator of the message at one stage, only to become the receptor at the next stage when the other party gives feedback on what had been earlier shared. In essence, Systems Theory shows that each communicating party is important and the contribution of each cannot be dispensed with towards effective dialogue.

A Look at Other Theories Buttressing Systems Theory

Having said that Systems Theory arose from the biological sciences even though it has found a place in the social sciences, this theory can also be understood through Functional Theory, which attempts an explanation of a phenomenon from the sociological perspective. Functionalism, as the theory is otherwise called, emerged in Europe in the nineteenth century as a response to perceived crises of the social order resulting from both the Industrial and French Revolution.

Functionalism holds that society is a complex system whose various parts work together to produce stability and solidarity (Giddens, 2001: 16). It accounts for the presence of an attribute in terms of its role in the operation of some process in maintaining the wellbeing of some entity (Pavitt, 1999: 315). Functionalism focuses on social systems as a whole: how they operate, the social consequences they produce, and the realization of the cultural values on which the system is based. Its proponents include August Comte, Emile Durkheim, Talcott Parsons, Robert Merton, and Max Weber to mention but a few.

In the study of small group communication and, by extension, dialogue, Functionalism is concerned with explaining how interaction affects group outcomes, especially the quality of decisions and how solutions can best be proffered to problems (Gouran, 1999: 15). In this light, Poole affirms that, "The result of functional theory and research is an understanding of how communication contributes to group effectiveness" (1999: 42).

A group is said to have two main functions: Maintenance/survival and task performance. The first function, maintenance, requires group cohesion and necessitates the enactment of communicative acts. These communicative acts perform positive socio-emotional functions like releasing tension, stating agreement, and showing solidarity with other group members. The second, survival, involves communicative acts like giving and asking for information, suggestions, and opinions. It is said that a contradiction may result in the maintenance and task goals of the group and that the way to ensure equilibrium is to have a leadership that will combine these two major functions of the group (Pavitt, 1999: 317).

Building on Systems and Functional theories, the academic discourse on dialogue can also be examined through an understanding of how people in dialogue employ certain symbols in communication and how better understanding of such symbols enhances the dialogue process. This was developed from the thought of John Dewey and William James who believed that reality is not objective but subjectively constructed. Following this argument, George H. Mead is said to have espoused Symbolic Interaction Theory.

The thrust of Symbolic Interaction Theory is that human beings redefine shared meanings in their environment. As people engage in dialogue, they use words and non-verbal symbols that convey a variety of meanings. The way persons are able to ascribe meanings to certain acts and behavior goes a long way in determining the kind of sharing taking place between them. For this to happen, persons in dialogue are encouraged to share common symbols that enhance the interpretation of such symbols. For example, people from Western parts of the world are taught to engage in dialogue while looking straight into the eyes of the other party. Failure to do this might be interpreted as not being truthful or that the person is timid.

On the contrary, to dialogue with an elder/senior, for example, in the African context entails not looking straight at the person's face. To do so would be taken as a sign of disrespect. The elder in the African cultural milieu is taken to be the repository of knowledge and, according to traditional culture, looking straight into his or her eyes during a conversation may be construed as challenging his/her authority. As such, the way both the Western person and his or her African counterpart engage eye contact in dialogue will influence the meaning they make out of the whole process. Thus, symbols are better understood when people's culture and their view of reality are taken into consideration.

This notion of Symbolic Interaction Theory has been broadened by another theory known as Social Construction Theory, which holds that "meaning does not reside inside one person's head, waiting to be shared with another. Rather, meaning exists in the practice of communication between people" (Turner & West, 2002: 61). This understanding helps persons in dialogue to know that sharing the same culture and worldview should be the first step towards building an effective communication process. These are the ingredients that help them to understand that no man or woman is an island, and that by sharing their individual ideas, they help to create a new meaning out of which everyone benefits.

Although Social Construction Theory emphasizes that people who share the same culture and worldview also share common symbols better, it also recognizes the importance of the communicating persons as active participants. This participatory approach has been regarded by Paulo Freire as "inter-subjectivity" (1981: 93). This is a situation whereby everyone engaged in the communication process is an actor – someone who is active and not passive. This means, in order to make meaning in the interaction of symbols, no one is to be looked down upon, and all are seen as co-creators of meaning.

This explains why communication is regarded as "a symbolic process in which human beings act to exchange perceptions and, ultimately to build the knowledge bank for themselves, one another, and society as a whole" (Stacks et al., 1991: 10). The symbols used in communication, in Freire's approach, bring about a better participation in those communicating since the symbols are created by the people themselves.

The use of stories, drama, and visual aids, to mention but a few, drive home the meaning of the message in contrast with mere speculations lacking a symbolic representation of what is being shared. Bornmann maintains through his Symbolic Convergence Theory that, by "dramatizing a message with the appropriate figure of speech, analogy, anecdote, parable, allegory, fable etc., all the world becomes a stage, and we are all actors at all times" (2003: 39-40).

This is seen in a special way in the African milieu where traditional means of bringing home truths about life include storytelling, music, drums, and symbolic language, to mention but a few. The importance of these to active participation in the process of dialogue stems from the fact that they are created by the participants, and everyone is involved in their use.

It is also pertinent to understand that Symbolic Interaction Theory has to do with the fact that human beings relate with others based on the meaning others have for them; meaning is created through interaction among people, and this meaning is modified as people interpret their interaction. Take for instance how social class determines who people relate with in society. Those who belong to the same social class share the same symbols easily, compared to someone from a different social class. For example, lawyers have their own language, and unless you belong there, you may not understand what they are saying. High-school students have their own ways of passing messages among themselves that the teacher or parent may not comprehend. Even for those within the same social class, as they interact, old ideas are either reinforced or rejected.

Of all the symbols people employ in communication, human language has the first place. How would you feel if, while you were in a foreign land where a different language is spoken, you happen to stumble on someone who speaks your native tongue? Should this happen, it is always a happy experience which gives one a sense of belonging and renewed identity, and may lead to a situation where the two parties begin to interact.

As the two of you interact, your behavior may undergo some changes. This is because, when people get to a foreign land where they don't speak the local language, the tendency is to withdraw from everyone and everything around them. You have a feeling of being lost in the crowd and anonymity sets in. However, when seeing someone who understands you, there is the tendency to loosen up. Here, as people interact, they shape their horizon and affect each other's perspectives on reality. In essence, the Systems Theory and other theories espoused here are vital to understanding how to bring about effective dialogue among communicating persons.

Experiential Application of the Theories

The scientific theories examined above have bearing on every aspect of daily life, as I earlier stated in the opening pages of this chapter. Personally, I see an expression of Systems Theory in the combination of my experience of the Christian faith, my culture as an African, and my education in Group Communication Studies. Among others, the Christian faith is built on the Gospel of Jesus Christ, who came to teach how people are connected with one another and with God. He started his public ministry by affirming what Isaiah (60:1) had earlier prophesied by saying he had been given the Spirit with which he is called to minister to all – the poor, the blind, the oppressed, etc. (Lk. 4:18).

Through his words and deeds, he reminded people of their interconnectedness through the golden rule, "Do unto others as you would have them to do to you." His mission was carried on among the early Christians, as Paul reminds his listeners of what Christ did to establish peace by breaking down the barriers of separation between slaves and the free, while at the same time teaching people how connected they are to one another (Eph. 2:14). This was put into practical expression as the early Church lived out the *koinonia*, that is, a communal living through which nothing is held in sole possession by anyone; rather, they all shared their belongings and catered to the needs of each one (Acts 4:32).

The same tenet of interconnectedness is expressed in the Church today through Small Christian Communities. Starting from Latin America where the small communities emerged as a way of marrying socio-cultural and political realities with the religious experience of Catholics, this expression of the Church as communion has been replicated all over the world. In Africa, the Church as small communities resonates with the culture where the personhood of an individual finds its true expression when lived within the community with others. The interconnectedness of life in traditional African culture is reflected in the saying, "I am because we are, and because we are, therefore, I am."

Backed by this Christian understanding of the human person and African culture, my education in human communication has been enriched through the understanding of the fact that the human person is a system, and those engaged in the communication process are vital components of this system. The understanding of homeostasis through Systems Theory buttresses the feedback aspect of the communication process, in which people do not just take in whatever is shared by others, but also give back what they have been able to digest in the process, and as such, maintain an equilibrium that sustains the process.

In the 20 years of my priestly ministry, I have seen how the faith experience of an individual can either make or mar that of others. Immediately after my priestly ordination in 2001, I served as a priest at St. Mary's Cathedral, Ibadan, under the then Cathedral Administrator Very Rev. Fr. T.O.A. Fadeyi. Back then, the Cathedral parish was given the responsibility of ministering to the pastoral needs of St. Mulumba Church, Alakia, and St. Julius Church, Aba Oni.

These two churches are geographically far from the Cathedral parish, which was situated in the heart of the city of Ibadan, and as such, each time either of us priests was to go to either of the two outstations, he needed to set out quite early. The Church in Aba Oni was so named after one of the first priests to be ordained in South-Western Nigeria, Msgr. Julius Oni, whose family hails from that part of the State. In fact, the village was named after his family, since Aba Oni simply means "Oni's village".

St. Julius Church, situated in Oni village, had many parishioners who were non-natives; many of them came to Aba Oni from Benue State, a North-Central part of Nigeria, for the sole purpose of farming. In this local community, the people were very close to nature. They lacked the basic necessities like good roads, electricity, or a hospital. Each trip to this community always ended up with a visit to the mechanic to fix one part or the other in the car. Despite the situation of these people, it was always a joy to be among them, and I always longed for when it would be my turn to go there for Mass. The joy that radiates in their faces, especially the children of this community, cannot be quantified.

In this community, there was man named John, who was not the catechist but acted like the life-wire of the community. Each Sunday, when we went for Mass in this village, together with John, we would go round the community jingling a little bell and calling everyone for Mass. What stood out for me about John was the fact that he was just like the rest of the people and was not obliged in any way to do everything he did, but he was there each time we went for Mass, organizing and engaging his peers. John had so much influence on the rest of the community that many of his fellow paid laborers saw no excuse not to be at Mass if John, who was one of them, could put in all this effort.

One day, I could not resist asking John what gave him the drive for all he did. John explained to me that he had been on the wrong side of life before he came across a priest in his part of the country who helped give his life a new and positive direction. He said he wished he could give back to the community just a little bit more, due to the immense blessings he has received from God. In this story of John and how he affected his community, one sees how interconnected we all can be. John brought his past experience to life in this small community and, his example of faith became a model for everyone around him.

In the academic field, I have also seen a manifestation of the fact that human life is a system where people are interdependent on many fronts. I have had the privilege of lecturing at various universities for a number of years. While some think the work of a lecturer is just to go to the classroom and dish out instructions to students, my experience of teaching shows that, to be effective, the teacher, as much as possible, needs to take the extra step of positively bringing about an integral development of the students. In my capacity as a lecturer, I have had the privilege of sharing in the stories, struggles, and successes of many students.

In one of the universities where I had lectured was a certain student named Clare. Clare came from a humble home and was the first child of her parent's six children. Being the eldest child in her part of Nigeria requires much responsibility. After her secondary school education, she was told not to proceed to the university but to get married so she could support her parents in the training of her siblings.

In their part of Nigeria, marriage was an easy way to better life for the family. As such, parents ensured their girl children married men who were wealthy. Sometimes, such marriages have many challenges. At any rate, Clare, having passed her secondary school examinations with flying colors, was determined to proceed to university, study hard, and get good grades so that upon graduation, she could be in a better position to assist her family after procuring a good job.

The aforesaid was not an easy choice for Clare since many suitors came calling and the pressure from the parents was unrelenting. Clare spoke to one of her uncles about her predicament, and he promised to sponsor her university education. So, she found herself in the university. What first caught my attention was the dedication of this young woman. She passed all her courses with flying colors.

Back then, we used to have a period in the Group Communication class in which students were divided into groups and asked to share their experiences of how they got into the program and their plans for the future. Although sharing was not compulsory, an appropriate level of disclosure was recommended each time we engaged in this exercise. It was in the process of sharing her experience that Clare made it known to the class the hurdle she had to overcome in order to participate in the program.

The group sharing that was done at the start of the program was always replicated at the conclusion of their time in the university. This was done to see if they had met the targets they set for themselves at the beginning of the program. It was during this summative evaluation that one of the students got up from her seat, walked straight to Clare, shook her hand, and thanked her for giving her the encouragement not only to continue with the program but to see it to the end. The name of this other student who thanked Clare was Jane.

Jane narrated how the experience shared by Clare four years ago had been the turning point in her own life. Unlike Clare, Jane came from an affluent family, and over the years, she had everything at her beck and call. Coming to the university was not her idea, but that of her parents since she saw no need to disturb herself with school owing to the luxuries her parents lavished on her already and the thoughts of a big inheritance at her disposal. On the day Clare shared her story with the class, however, Jane went back into her hostel thinking how blessed she was without knowing it. She wept for not taking her opportunities seriously and made a determination that day not to take her educational pursuit for granted.

The day Jane shared her testimony with the class, the silence in the room was palpable upon hearing what she had bottled up in the last four years, and Clare was herself taken aback. For four years, Clare had had no idea how the story she shared about her struggles went a long way to positively affect the life of someone else. As the lecturer, this was an opportunity for me to remind them all that education is not just about what the teacher lectures in the classroom, but that the school is a system where everything and everyone is interconnected and interdependent.

This was made evident in the story of these two young women who are now employed after their university education. As it is now, Clare is able to support her parents in the education of her siblings, and Jane has become not just the pride of her parents, but most importantly, she now sees the need not to rely on their wealth but to engage herself in building a better future as an individual.

As the experiences narrated above attest, Systems Theory can be applied to every aspect of life since it deals with nothing more than the interconnectedness of the human person. Human beings are social by nature and no one is an island unto himself or herself. Human history has pointed out the fact that people in prehistoric times lived by depending on one another through trade by barter. It is said that back in those days, people who had salt, exchanged it with another person who had oil, in order to make soup. Although each maintained whatever was produced in their individual communities, they shared the end product with others and were also ready to receive from other people.

Systems Theory, Globalization, and Development Communication

In more recent times, globalization has again buttressed the interconnectedness of humanity, since goods and services are moved around the globe thanks to the advent of the Internet, which brought unprecedented ease to communication, transportation, and commerce. Some have questioned the movement engendered by the globalizing effort of developed nations since, oftentimes, this effort is like one-way traffic; that is, a movement from Western nations to the rest of the world without a corresponding and reciprocal readiness to accept the culture and other aspects of life that developing nations might offer to the global discourse. In present times, people continue to lament the fact that globalization is measured in terms of dollars and cents, while values, cultures, and people's way of life are sacrificed on the altar of capitalism. This has been a prolonged argument in development studies.

The aspect of Communication Studies that examines development is known as Communication for Development or Development Communication. This seeks to understand the communication model that favors how a people come to a better understanding of themselves and their environment so as to tell their own story and share their experiences with the rest of the world. This is very important since, as mentioned above, Western strategies propagated economic growth, technical modernization, and increased productivity that brought prosperity to their communities and presented the same strategies as the instruments for transforming traditional pre-modern societies into economies that resembled their own (Boren, 1994: 17). Development Communication shows that this effort began after the Second World War, as former colonial territories were gaining independence and charting paths for their own futures.

Some of the theories that emerged at this time are Modernization, Dependency, Diffusion of Innovation, and Alternative Model of Development. Modernization theory presents development as linear and suggests that it must be uniform in all societies. Development was seen here as: "...mapping and making, it was about the spatial reach of power and control and management of other peoples, territories, environment, and places" (Crush, 1995: 7).

The social and political milieu at that time was rife with the distinction between development and underdevelopment to the extent that the local people were compelled to look at themselves as completely underdeveloped and having nothing to offer the rest of the world. The role communication played at this time cannot be over-emphasized. The only means of reaching the public at this time was the mass media of newspaper, radio, and television. These were owned and controlled mainly by the government. They had no capacity for dialogue or feedback from the people. As such, the media followed the hypodermic notion of communication as a means of influencing and controlling people.

Another theory that was used to explain development and how this should flow among people at this time is known as Dependency

Theory. As the name suggests, this is a view of development that sees developing nations as relying on developed nations. This is a conditioning situation in which the development of one nation is conditioned by that of the other. In the economic field, agricultural production at this time was concentrated on a particular product that was in high demand by developed nations. This was the period when Nigeria, for example, recorded a high level of cocoa exportation at the expense of other areas of agriculture. The raw materials were purchased at low cost but the finished products came back to the country as beverages at exorbitant prices.

Mumbengegwi holds that there was an effort at superimposition of agricultural practices by developed nations on traditional ones through: "...physical and political coercion of African peasants, legislative discrimination, and a host of direct economic measures designed to disadvantage the indigenous farmers vis-a-vis the white settlers" (1986: 203). The dependency that was forced on people in the field of agriculture is also seen at an alarming rate after the discovery of oil, for example, in Nigeria.

The discovery of oil, first in the Oloibiri community, in the South-South part of Nigeria and now in many parts of Nigeria, which was supposed to be a blessing for the people, has become a major bane economically and in the area of health and security. Many of the communities where crude oil is drilled in Nigeria suffer untold hardship, while the multinational companies who run the show smile to the banks. In many of these communities, the water is polluted, the roads are impassable, and the corresponding health hazard is unimaginable.

Connected to Modernization and Dependency theories, the Diffusion of Innovation Theory also tried to explain development in relation to developed and developing nations of the world. This theory is concerned with the impact of the media in projecting Western ideas on the rest of the world. Thus, "the role of communication was to transfer technological innovations from development agencies to their clients and to create an appetite for change through raising a climate for modernization among the members of the public" (Rogers, 1986: 49). This approach places emphasis on the effects of communication, that is, the ability of media messages and opinion leaders to create knowledge of new practices and ideas.

The ability is consolidated by persuading the target audience to adopt the ideas coming from outside. Adoption is the degree to which an individual accepts or rejects the innovation. The process of making a choice to adopt goes through five stages: awareness, interest, evaluation, trial, and adoption. This can be explained in the sense that when an innovation is introduced, one gets to know about it (awareness), this creates the curiosity to know more about the innovation (interest), then one begins to ask if this is truly what one needs or not (evaluation). It is after a period of evaluation that one tries out what has just been introduced (trial), and the final stage is when one decides to accept this new idea or not (adoption).

In the same vein, adopters can be grouped into five levels with increasing capacity for adoptability: innovators, early adopters, early majority, late majority, and laggards. As lofty as the idea of diffusion of innovation sounds, the main criticism of this approach is its lack of dialogue. Rather, it has the attribute of controlling and influencing others without any input from the latter. Since media is used to a large extent in this regard, it has been faulted for over-using its power to transform people, without giving consideration to the content of media messages or to the input of local people in formulating such messages.

People's undue dependence on the media through this approach also created a big divide between the info-rich and info-poor. This is a situation whereby those who have more access to the media possess more information and are said to be info-rich, in contrast to others who, maybe due to social status, income, or location, have little or no access to the means of diffusing the innovation and are then said to be info-poor. The main gist here is the fact that diffusion of innovation is roundly faulted since it is not dialogical, but only serves the interest of a few over the majority of others who are made mere receptors of media messages.

Having seen the limitations of the theories of development examined above and how they fail to meet the standard of Systems Theory in affirming the interconnectedness and interrelationship that should occur among people as they engage in the globalizing effort, this book underscores the importance of the Alternative Model of Development Theory since it is in tandem with the tenets of Systems Theory. This is an offshoot of popular culture, which began in the 1970s, as one of the ways of achieving developmental initiatives that start with decision-making at the grassroots level of small groups and communities.

In place of the former approaches where decisions were made for the people, this method involves people in the process of identifying their problems and proffering solutions in a dialogical way. Here, development is seen as a process that is not top-to-bottom but bottom-up. That is, development becomes social change with the main goal of improvement in the quality of life of all people by making them the masters of their own destiny. To achieve this, everyone must be actively involved, and participation is not just a means, but an end in itself. Here, everyone sees himself or herself as an integral part of the whole, who must function to maintain equilibrium. This is the idea behind Systems Theory.

Unlike in Modernization, Dependency, or Diffusion of Innovation, the Alternative Model shows how dialogue is a vital aspect of human life, which favors participation and dialogue. It is pluralistic in approach, and the media are to be used democratically here, not as means of influencing recipients of media messages. Many nations in Latin America, Africa, and Asia have, at various times, employed this approach of using small group media like pictures, stories, drawings, drama, etc. to bring about active participation among people in local groups as they address deep-seated problems in their communities.

Examples of the dialogical dimension espoused in Systems Theory can be found in the moonlight tales and the story of Moremi I mentioned in the first chapter of this book. The grass-roots dimension of this approach shows how it values the culture and way of life of a people and how this should be taken into consideration in the cross-pollination of ideas which globalization should foster in a real sense. As such, this chapter has been about giving a theoretical base to the discourse through Systems Theory. By understanding communication as a process that begins with a sender, goes to the receiver and, through feedback, the process is recycled; this chapter of the book holds that everyone involved in this meaning-making process is important to the system and should be given the rightful place therein.

CHAPTER THREE

———•———

Listening: A Vital Aspect of Dialogue

It is said that there is a reason humans have two ears but one mouth. Some persons have said this is to enable us to listen more, but speak less. Whichever way you may wish to look at it, listening is not just an important aspect of the communication process but of the entire gamut of human relationships. The process of listening demands that we "not only hear the words, but also embrace, accept, and gradually let go of our own inner clamoring. As we explore it, we discover that listening is an expansive activity" (Isaacs, 2010: 91). The sense of hearing is very vital and very distinct from all other senses because you cannot shut it out.

One may decide to close one's eyes so as not to see something, hold one's breath to avoid perceiving a foul odour, refuse to touch or be touched in order to avoid the sense of feel, or refuse to taste something, no matter how delicious. However, no one can close his/her ears from hearing. Even when we practice selective hearing by choosing to concentrate on one out of the many sounds around us, it is obvious that we are still bombarded daily with different sounds begging for our attention. Since listening is not limited to hearing just sounds, scholars hold different but converging views on what it takes to have an effective listening process and its place in the process of dialogue.

Isaacs (2010) holds that for a listening process to be effective: one needs to be conscious of one's own thoughts, which helps to bring out ideas from within the person; one must concentrate on the fact of the matter because other ideas may cross one's mind, but the need to stay focused is paramount; and there is need to be conscious of the ladder of inference through which we learn to make a distinction between what we judge an issue to be and what it really is in itself. This is to avoid coming to hasty conclusions, which may end up being false.

There is also the need to note the disturbance that occurs while listening to people and finding ourselves immersed in our own past issues. Isaacs suggests that in this situation, we follow disturbance by beginning to focus on what triggers us and look for what really makes us uncomfortable in the dialogue as a way of getting to know how others feel when we engage them in conversation. Isaacs concludes that by listening without resistance and standing still, we may become aware of what could stand in the way of our listening to others and thus silence the inner turbulence within us and realize that there is another world out there worth exploring.

Listening becomes hard when those engaged in communication do not use the same cues or when one fails to understand symbols used by the other. One of the first shocks I got when I newly arrived in Rome for my doctoral studies was the symbol people used when saying goodbye, that is, "Ciao". This word is usually accompanied by the wave of a cupped-hand facing the outside, as if the person is beckoning the other as it would indicate in Africa. I still remember with nostalgia, lots of memories of the experiences I had in those early months in the eternal city, as Rome is fondly called. One of such experience was one day, as I was leaving the lecture hall after a tedious day of multi-tasking (making serious effort to understand Italian language while at the same time trying so hard to understand what is being taught with that language), the lecturer said "Ciao" to me with a wave of the hand.

Thinking the lecturer needed me, I came back towards him and was surprised at the look on his face, seeing me standing in front of him. The good thing is, although the official language of the school is Italian, many of the lecturers understood a minimum of four other languages, English included. As such, he switched into English and gently asked why I was standing in front of him. I muttered in the little Italian I could gather at the time, *"Mi Ha chiamato,"* that is, "You called me." He simply smiled but was able to decipher my confusion. He said, "When the Italian waves with the hand as I just did, while saying Ciao, they actually mean "Goodbye". I quickly pointed out that, in my part of the world, such a wave of the hand signals and beckons someone to come.

Another of such experiences happened in my residence in Rome. This is a college that houses students from different parts of the world. After each day at school, we gathered around the dinner table to discuss how the day went for each of us. I vividly remember how, one day, a friend of mine came to the dinner table looking dejected and sad. When we probed to know what the matter was, he expressed frustration concerning what he had experienced that day at school. He lamented how the lecturer taught them Latin using Italian language. He said jokingly, "The Italian, I do not even understand and now he (the lecturer) was using a language I do not understand to teach me another foreign language." We had a good laugh at this outburst from our friend.

Universities in Rome encouraged and even demanded that new foreign students arrive in Italy months before the commencement of the academic year so they could go to a language school and also learn about Italian culture. In fact, there were students from Korea, China, and other nations where people do not write with alphabets, who arrive in Italy a year or two early just to study the Italian language before commencing their university studies. Despite these efforts of the universities to help students grasp the Italian language, oftentimes it is a work in progress for many students.

Personally, in my early months in Rome, on many occasions, I joined others in laughter when the lecturer cracked a joke in the course of teaching without my having the minutest knowledge of what the joke was about. One day, I asked another student sitting beside me in the class what the joke was all about. He simply shrugged and said: "I don't know, I saw people laugh and simply did the same." We both had a good laugh at that!

Scholars have emphasized the importance of cultural presuppositions in the communication process. This is not only the premise within which communication occurs, but it is what gives structure and form to social organizations (Baraldi, 2009; Weizman, 2008). When a communication cue is misunderstood due to cultural differences, listening and meaning-making become hard nuts to crack. This was the situation in my encounter with my teacher in the experience narrated above. There are many other instances of cultural diversity and how such affected meaning-making in my early time in Italy.

Now, with a better understanding of Italian language, recalling such experiences can make one chuckle. Anyone who has had the opportunity of studying another language can identify with what is being said here. Imagine, for example, your first visit to Europe as a North American, whose main language is English, and the difficulty you would have had in putting the French, Italian, German, Spanish, or whatever European language you studied in high school into practice. I know of many Canadians who are proud of their European roots and make every effort to visit Europe when they can. If you look back at those earlier times from the perspective of whatever stage you are currently in with understanding that language, you can further identify with my experience in the first few months of my stay in Rome.

Listening is not as simple as it seems but, if done well, it enables everyone engaged in the meaning-making process to have a better grasp of what is being shared and give appropriate feedback (Geiman & Greene, 2019; Graham, 2011). A great percentage of our everyday life is spent listening even when we are not aware of that fact. As you are reading this book, you may be in the library, in your living room, on a bus, or in the park. Wherever you find yourself at this time, there are many things begging for your attention: a fellow library user turning pages of a book, the hum of a fan, the traffic on the road, or people walking around you. We are faced everyday with numerous and myriad activities beckoning for us to listen.

Apart from external factors seeking our attention, there are also myriad voices of inner dialogue that require our attention. As you read this book, you might be having the thought of finishing reading it in one stretch or getting up and going for lunch. Your thoughts might be revolving around what you need to do tomorrow or occupied with unfinished work in the office. We always have a lot of things vying for our attention, but even if we give some level of attention to most, we cannot surely listen to all. We hear all, but we listen to the one that appeals most to our interest at a particular point in time.

There is a great difference between hearing and listening. In listening to that which appeals to our interest, we practice what is called selective hearing. As such, when confronted with many sounds on the outside or diverse thoughts on the inside, we choose which one to give priority. This choice-making is dependent on a lot of factors, including the importance of the item and our degree of interest in it. At any rate, the act of listening is differentiated from just hearing because, in listening, we make a commitment to filter out other things and concentrate on a particular item so as to better understand it and give an appropriate response to it.

Many people limit the act of listening to verbal communication. On the contrary, a great amount of communication occurs on the non-verbal level. Non-verbal cues are acts, which though not made up of speech, are also used to share meaning among human beings. The non-verbal means of communication has been defined as actions and artifactual cues that are not linguistic yet have meaningful effects. An adage says, "What you do speaks so loudly that I cannot hear what you say." As such, dimensions of non-verbal communication include paralanguage, kinesics, and proxemics. Before we examine each of the aforementioned aspects of non-verbal communication, it is important to note the extent that this aspect of communication is employed in day-to-day dialogue, even without us paying much attention to it.

I had earlier narrated an experience I had in Italy with the use of a wave of the hand, which brought confusion due to cultural differences. The first function that non-verbal communication performs and which we shall examine here is "repeating". That was simply what my professor did by saying "Ciao" and with a wave of his hand. Imagine when someone does something that thrills you, and you find yourself saying, "Good job", while at the same time making the thumbs-up sign to accompany what you just said. In this case, the non-verbal clue of thumbs up repeats what you had actually said verbally.

Just as a non-verbal sign can repeat what is said, it can also contradict verbal communication. This occurs when the tone of voice or facial expression does not correspond with what is said verbally. Imagine those times when you engaged in sarcasm! You spoke in praise of someone while your face and tone actually showed the contrary. Apart from the two mentioned uses of non-verbal signs, they can also be used instead of spoken words. Although using non-verbal clues in place of words can bring about misunderstanding, as I earlier showed in the chapter that examined symbolic interaction, for those who share the same sign, it is a potent way of sharing ideas. Many children are brought up to know whether to receive gifts or not from strangers by simply looking at their mothers' faces.

I remember as a child, each time we had visitors at home, we need not be told to leave the living room (even in the middle of an interesting TV program), since with a simple stare from my parents the message would have been passed. Apart from substituting the spoken word, non-verbal communication is also used to accent and regulate what is being said. With accent, your tone of voice could either show respect or contempt for the person you are in dialogue with, and the use of a head nod or body movement during dialogue can indicate whether you want the speaker to continue or that you are bored and he/she needs to stop talking. All these uses of non-verbal communication can be seen in the different aspects of non-verbal communication, which we shall now examine one after the other, beginning with paralanguage.

Paralanguage

Between the act of making a sound by a sender and understanding such a verbal sign by the receiver, a lot of activities go on within the communicator. George Trager (1961) and other scholars in this field of study have identified a wide variety of vocal qualities like timbre and tempo; vocal qualifiers like intensity and extent; vocal characterizers like throat clearing; and vocal segregates like hum, err, and other intruding sounds. Vocal qualities are created by the physical process of speech production, and they can be divided into inflection, timbre, rate, and control.

Inflection concerns the changes in pitch and loudness in the voice. Pitch and loudness in the voice are often indications that someone is sure of what he or she is saying and is bold enough to express such an idea. The same is not true of someone who is unsure of himself or herself. You sometimes see this in elementary school settings where the kids shout at the top of their voice when they know what they are saying to the teacher while, on the other hand, they tend to speak inaudibly and sometimes gaze at their toes when not so sure about the topic of discussion.

Timbre has to do with the "fullness" or resonance of the voice, for example, the clarity you get on your FM radio stations in contrast to the short-wave frequency, which most times has some form of background noise. Rate deals with the tempo or speed of speech. Studies show that most people talk at an average rate of about 125 words per minute. In dialogue, it is often noticed that people tend to talk faster when they are either angry or overjoyed.

Imagine seeing a friend you have not seen for a long period of time. You are tempted to talk fast as you wish to catch up and tell the person almost everything within a few seconds. Now, contrast that with a situation where someone feels sadness. The rate of speech is not only slowed but also choked up due to crying in extreme sadness. Control is the last factor here, and it has to do with the smoothness of the movements of the lips and tongue. This is most visible when one is happy or afraid. As such, this movement communicates something deeper that only the person with a secondary level of listening can decipher.

Vocal qualifiers produce meanings in the paralanguage study, which help in understanding how a speaker employs the verbal communication cues of intensity and extent. For example, the differences between an angry voice and a sad one can be deduced in the sense that an angry voice has irregular inflection, a fast rate, loud volume, a high pitch, and clipped enunciation. On the other hand, a sad voice has downward inflection, a slow rate, reduced loudness, and a low pitch. As such, the way one's voice is qualified in dialogue tells more than the spoken word. It takes someone who is able to listen beyond the spoken word to understand the state of mind of the other person in dialogue and the appropriate feedback to give in different contexts.

A vocal characterizer is expressed through certain mannerisms when speaking. Although some have medical issues, which affect the projection of voice thereby making them clear their throat every now and then, some others believe that clearing the throat when speaking comes with old age. As such, hearing the voice of someone who clears their throat periodically, especially if the speakers are not communicating face-to-face, can make one assume that the speaker is elderly. The act of clearing the throat is rampant in many African countries where elders couch their speeches in parables and anecdotes, and take their time in voicing whatever they have to say. To speak without clearing the throat or to rush through statements could be perceived as not living up to the standard of an elder in the community.

The same is true of vocal segregates. As the name suggests, these are used in dialogue to break the flow of thought. Many persons have the mannerism of dousing their speeches with things like "hum", "err", etc. The use of these can be interpreted as someone who is unsure of what he or she wants to say and so uses segregates to buy time and think out the points. The Yorubas of Nigeria have a saying, *"Ai gbo'fa la nwoke, ifa kan ko si ni para."* This simply translates that one only wastes time when such a person is not certain of what to do or say. If one is certain, you are ready to channel out your point of view as quickly and succinctly as possible. Therefore, paralanguage helps us understand that to listen is not just to understand the words people speak, but also and most importantly, listening involves other aspects of speech which, though non-verbal, go a long way to give meaning to what is being said verbally in a process of dialogue.

Kinesics

The act of listening is not limited to the spoken word or the non-verbal cues used in communication. For instance, there have been times in Nigeria when certain government agents carried out certain actions, and when asked on whose authority such acts were performed, most times they only say, "The body language of the boss indicated that is what we should do." There have been times when those agents' actions had dire consequences or involved gross violation of people's rights, but to the dismay of all, often nothing was done to checkmate their wrong deeds. In essence, they might not be wrong in saying that they based their judgment on the perceived body language of their boss.

A case in view is the incarceration of Omoyele Sowore, the New York-based Nigerian journalist and convener of the "RevolutionNow" movement in Nigeria. Sowore was arrested in August 2019 by the Department of State Security (DSS) on the premise that, having failed in his 2019 Presidential election bid, he then called for revolution to topple the elected government. Opinions differ on this, however, since, owing to joblessness, insecurity, and poverty in the land, many feel the government has failed in its duty to protect lives and properties and provide the basic necessities for the citizenry. Hence, they hold that taking part in an election and not winning should not stop a concerned citizen from raising concerns on the state of affairs in a nation.

At any rate, upon Sowore's arrest, the court ordered that he should be kept in DSS custody for a period of 45 days. At the expiration of the initial injunction and after spending many months in detention, the court granted him bail, but he was not released by the DSS. Even after his bail conditions were met and the court was sitting to hear his case, security operatives, allegedly from the DSS, stormed the courtroom in Abuja to re-arrest him. This act by the DSS and the mayhem it caused has been described as a travesty of justice and a desecration of the hallowed chambers of jurisprudence. This act was frowned on by almost everyone in the legal profession and even ordinary Nigerians condemned this blatant disregard for the court of justice.

Despite national and international outcry which decried this act by the security operatives, not even one of those security operatives has been brought to book at the time of writing this book. Part of the international outcry was by Sowore's wife, who together with the member of the United States Congress for his constituency in New York and many other interest groups called for his release. Sowore was later released from prison but he was ordered not to leave the Federal Capital territory, not to talk of traveling abroad to visit his family.

As it is often said in Nigeria, officers of the DSS were said to be acting based on the body language of their boss. This was also the case when the same Sowore was rearrested on December 31, 2020, on the streets of Abuja while peacefully protesting against the incarceration of other protesters who were arrested by the Nigerian government during the #ENDSARS protest in October,

2020. As illustrated by the above episode, the human body has its own language, which needs to be listened to in the process of communication so as to avoid engaging in acts which can result from incorrect interpretation of it.

Kinesics is that aspect of communication study that deals with body language (Birdwhistell, 1955, 1991; Jolly, 2000). Scholars in this field claim eight different body elements can be used to communicate various things. These are the: head, face, neck, trunk, shoulder-arm-wrist, hand, hip-joint-leg-ankle, and foot. For the purpose of this book, these shall be grouped into two broad categories of facial expressions and body behavior. Facial expression is very important in face-to-face communication, which we all engage in on a daily basis. When we engage in dialogue in an interpersonal context, we use facial expression to a large extent. The face expresses a considerable variety of emotions with ease.

The dominant feature of the face is the eyes, and a great deal of communication is made through the eyes. Eye contact is essential not just as a way of beginning a dialogue but also as a way of seeking feedback from the other person. Imagine yourself at a bus or train station and needing to ask directions from a stranger; the first thing you do is look at the person. If the person looks back at you and maybe offers a smile, you are more at ease to make your request. On the contrary, if the person refuses to look in your direction or looks at you and, with a frown, turns away, you are prone to look for a more friendly face to make your request. In the same token, prolonged eye contact can bring about a feeling of discomfort in people and may be interpreted as a sign of hostility.

As I mentioned earlier in this book, eye contact has cultural connotations. Most Africans are trained not to look at an elder straight in the eye since this may be interpreted as a sign of disrespect, while in Western cultures, avoiding eye contact might signify that the person is not telling the truth or is being timid due to some past bad experience. With regard to body behavior, people have been classified along the lines of: endomorphs (soft, round, heavy figures), who are said to be older, shorter, more talkative, sympathetic, and dependent; mesomorphs (bony, muscular, athletic figure), who are believed to be stronger, younger, taller, mature, and self-reliant; and ectomorphs (tall, thin, fragile-looking), who are seen to be younger and ambitious.

In all this, the way people perceive your body make-up can condition the way they listen to you. Height, body posture, and the way you move can all communicate something about you to others. Some persons can be taken to be proud just because of the way they walk. I was talking with a lady recently who lamented how people see her to be imposing just because she is tall. According to her, some persons think she is proud simply on account of her height.

Most times, it is not really about the person, but how others choose to interpret the body build of other persons and how this affects the communication between them. Thus, it is important for people in dialogue to listen to each other, not just through the spoken word, but also by paying close attention to the kinesics aspect of communication, since bodily movement can send a lot of messages. This will, among others, guard against the wrong interpretation of body language, for instance, by the security operatives in the example I cited above.

Proxemics

This has to do with the impact of spatial relationships on communication with others. This is important, since human beings tend to have a sense of territoriality, that is, each one seems to claim a space for himself/herself. I once heard of a certain gentleman who attended a particular parish church for many years. For all those years, he sat at a particular spot in the church, and everyone in the parish knew that to be his spot. As such, no one dared sit in that particular spot. His friends sometime tried to poke fun at him by arriving early to church and sitting in that spot. However, immediately when he arrived and gave the "look", they would smile, stand up, and go to another spot in the church.

There came a day when the parish organized a program that brought lots of people from within and outside the community together. The visitors to the church sat wherever they found an open space. The gentleman of the parish later came and, to his surprise, there was someone sitting in his beloved spot. He looked at the person and smiled. The person, taking him to be one of the greeters simply smiled back. He looked again and smiled. The visitor was becoming uncomfortable but also smiled back. Since he was still standing there, the guest looked up and this time saw a big frown on this man's face. The guest simply looked away while remaining seated in the same spot.

Without saying any word, the gentleman from the parish stormed out of the church and went home. He could not understand why someone would have the audacity to occupy his cherished spot, which he had maintained over the years to the knowledge of everyone in his church. We may not be as dramatic as this gentleman, but we all share something with him. That is, if we constantly go to a particular place, be it church, a meeting place, the library, etc., we tend to choose certain places to sit time and time again. Although we may not say anything if, for some reason, we find someone else in our cherished spot, we often do not feel happy that our spot has been taken. In this simple act, we communicate something about the use of space. In Communication Studies, the use of space in communication can be examined through distance and placement.

With regard to distance, Edward Hall (1963, 1976) says we create at least four different zones of communication: intimate, personal, social, and public. These various kinds of distances affect what we say and how we say it. The intimate distance is reserved for telling secrets and the volume is generally softer and lower in this zone. The personal distance is between 18 inches to 4 feet and is where interpersonal communication takes place. The level of the voice is normal, that is, neither loud nor too soft, for those communicating within this zone.

The social distance ranges from 4 to 10 feet, and this is a group distance where discussions are normally non-personal and the voice is loud and clear. The public distance goes from 10 to 22 feet and the voice needs to be projected so the whole group can hear. It is important to consider the space within which one is communicating and the meaning such use of space communicates. If the tone and level of voice meant for the social space is used at the intimate level, then one begins to decipher a problem; that is, why is one person shouting at another? Moreover, other factors that influence the use of space include gender, status, relationship, etc.

With regard to gender, there is a level of distance that is maintained between people of the same gender without which a wrong meaning may be adduced to their interaction. Imagine two strangers of the complementary gender, meeting for the first time at a bus station and taking a position at an intimate distance. This would be unusual because they are not known to each other, and they are in a public space. While it may be possible for a guy meeting another guy or a lady meeting another lady for the first time to keep some distance in an open space to discuss anything, such may be given a different interpretation if the people are of different genders.

The use of distance is also influenced by social status, since someone of a higher status is often given some level of distance when others of a lower status try to communicate with such a person. Think of the distance you put between your boss and yourself in juxtaposition with the distance between your friend and yourself when communicating. In the same light, relationship influences distance in the sense that those who share an intimate relationship can often be spotted holding hands while walking down the street. In essence, it is important to be aware of distance when dialoguing with people, since a wrong use of this aspect of communication can send a wrong signal, which may affect the entire communication process.

With regard to placement, we are often concerned with the way people are arranged within a given space. For example, those who take the head seat at the dinner table assume a certain position. In most homes, the father sits at the end of the table to signal the role he plays within the family. Robert Sommer (2002), an exponent in this field of study, conducted research into the relationship of spatial placement on human behavior and attitude. One of the early experiences that launched Sommer into this field was an experience he had while working in a mental hospital in Saskatchewan, in Western Canada in the 1950s.

Sommer noticed that the hospital was constructed with long corridors, which were poorly lit, and the ventilation was very poor. He came up with the question that, if the space within the hospital environment is not well situated to the needs of the patients and staff, how could it offer the healing it was meant to provide? He believed physical arrangement could enhance interaction, which would, in the long run, aid the staff in their work and help patients in the healing process. Thus, he claimed that the nature of the task influences seating preferences, since people prefer sitting across from one another for conversing, side by side for cooperating, and across from one another for working separately at the same task.

Other scholars have examined the import of spatial relationships from psychological and other perspectives (Coello & Fischer, 2015; Kennedy, Tyszka, et al., 2009). For these scholars, spatial placement communicates strong emotional messages. There is an ocean of difference in the emotional messages between a funeral context, for example, and what occurs at a wedding ceremony. This is because the emotions communicated in these two examples are diverse. One needs to listen to the context at hand in order to give an appropriate response to that context. Again, different environments require different spatial relationships; for example, consider the use of space in a church and a library, and the power dynamics at play in each of these places. The pews in a church are arranged in a way that people know the roles each person in the gathered assembly plays in that context – the pastor, the choir, the readers, etc.

Persons in a church setting have their roles specified by the kind of space they occupy in that context, which is not the same with the seating arrangement in a library. In the latter, chairs and tables are arranged with no specific roles in play. Each library user is just like the person beside him or her in terms of the power dynamic. In the same vein, Sommer believes social environments create quite different interaction patterns. For example, at the airport, rows of chairs are neatly arranged to separate the lounges, and this is distinct from the bars and shops. For example, because of the way chairs are placed in airports, you do not see the same kind of banter that might occur in the bar happening in an airport lounge.

One can better understand the need to listen to the form of communication that takes place in the use of space through the experience of Jimmy. Born of Haitian parentage, Jimmy has been living in Canada for the last three years. Jimmy shared with me an episode he encountered while living in his homeland. He was brought up in a Christian home and, due to the fact that Haitians share African heritage, respect for elders was a given in his family.

Jimmy was sent to a boarding school at a young age, where he had to reside with other high-school students. In this boarding school, students did a lot of things together, including having their meals together in a big refectory. They were therefore divided into groups of 10 students per table. On the first day of school, Jimmy joined other students to go for dinner in the school refectory. He saw an empty seat at the head of the table and sat, waiting to be served his portion of the meal.

The next thing he noticed was one of his seniors coming and asking him to stand up and kneel down throughout the period of the meal. The senior student told him the part of the table where he chose to sit was reserved for senior students alone. At this point, Jimmy became emotional and began to cry. When the senior student inquired why he chose to sit at the head of the table, Jimmy revealed he has a medical condition that makes him belch each time he eats. In order not to disturb other students on the table with the foul smell, he chose the extreme end of the table where he could easily turn his head away from others to pass out the gas.

The senior student felt bad for the way he had treated Jimmy, having thought that Jimmy had just been arrogant. He consoled the poor boy for the way he had treated him and took Jimmy as his school son from that day, ensuring none of the other senior students oppressed the boy. Many people can identify with Jimmy in the sense of finding themselves taking the wrong position at gatherings unknowingly. People have been tagged as proud, insolent, arrogant, etc., just because they unknowingly occupied the wrong space and thus communicated a wrong message to others. It is therefore important to be aware of the use of space and how placement communicates a great deal of things that might be not be perceived through verbal communication alone.

Dialogue and the Phases of Listening

Having explored the need to listen to non-verbal cues in communication, let us now turn our attention to the phases with which one can better engage in both the verbal and non-verbal aspects of communication so as to achieve better listening during dialogue. Authors differ on the various stages or phases of listening, but for the purpose of this book we shall be examining five phases of listening. These are: receiving (hearing and attending), understanding (learning and deciphering meaning), remembering (recalling and retaining), evaluating (judging and criticizing), and responding (answering/giving feedback).

Receiving is the first stage of listening where one focuses on the speaker's verbal and non-verbal messages, and that is why the main acts performed here are hearing and attending. That is, hearing what is said verbally but also attending to the non-verbal signs employed in the dialogue process. We have mentioned above how some of the non-verbal messages in the communication process can be polysemic, that is, having the tendency to be given different interpretations. As such, one needs to be actively engaged in receiving this kind of message. Since no communication occurs in a vacuum, but many factors, including noise, are part of the process, the reception aspect must avoid distractions in the environment.

I talked earlier of the noise in a library or on the road or an internal dialogue within the person, which can serve as noise in the communication process. All these are to be avoided if the receiving aspect of listening is to be effective. One other thing to do at this level is to focus attention on the speaker and not on what you will say next. You may have heard people say, "I know what you intend to say," or "I know where you are coming from in this conversation." This is because many of us spend a great amount of time planning what we want to say in response to what is being said, and thus we fail to really give the needed time to receive the message in the first place. In order to have an effective reception of the message, it is important to maintain your role as a listener without interrupting the speaker until he or she finishes.

Understanding is the next stage of listening, which deals with how we relate the speaker's new information to what we already know. Suffice to say, no one comes into any communication process *tabula rasa*, that is, empty. Each one possesses some form of knowledge based on past experience, education, culture, etc. These factors not only shape and condition how we listen, they also influence how we comprehend what is being said. Although we tend to relate our own past experiences to what we are listening to, we need to see the message from the speaker's point of view without superimposing our own views on it.

Many persons go into dialogue with a closed mind, and they are not able to separate their past knowledge on an issue from what new information they may be getting. It is recommended that dialogue be engaged in with an open mind. In case of doubt, we need to ask questions for clarification and rephrase the speaker's ideas to check on our understanding of the speaker's thoughts and feelings. Questions like, "Do you mean it was after you left the house that you saw him?" goes a long way to show that you are not only listening but you are also following the track of events. This encourages the speaker to know he or she is being followed in the dialogue and to supply the missing link in what you have just repeated.

Remembering is the stage of listening in which we try to identify the central ideas and the major themes advanced in a dialogue process. Every form of communication has certain ideas that stand out from others. As I earlier mentioned, we can hear everything that the communication process presents to us, but we actually listen to only some of the points. Thus, remembering is the ability to identify the main ideas in a dialogue.

The next thing to do after identifying the central points is to summarize the message in an easier-to-retain form. People do this in various ways. I remember in my graduate student days, we prepared for examinations by studying and writing main points in short notes, which we termed "made-easy". Made-easy are cogent points jotted on a small piece of paper, which you can fold and put into the pocket. You can read a whole book and put the points in each chapter into a "made-easy" format, which you could easily carry around.

In the case of a conversation or dialogue, the "made-easy" can be the names or key concepts you have heard, which you can repeat to yourself silently or aloud if appropriate. If this is a formal talk with a recognizable organizational structure, identify this structure and use it to organize what the speaker is saying. Discussions about health, economy, or technology will have different salient points, and the ability to identify the structure of each discourse helps a great deal in organizing one's point. The main gist in remembering is to dissect what is being heard into cogent points and have the ability to retain those points in memory for easy recall much later.

Evaluating is the next stage of listening, which we all engage in, though in various capacities. Oftentimes we engage in premature evaluation and lose track of what is being said. This is caused by a lot of factors including a bias or prejudice we may have about the topic or speaker. Earlier, we examined how body makeup is used to judge people. People who are short in stature have sometimes been stereotyped to act in certain ways while those who are plump are sometimes said to behave in another manner. We also sometimes judge people based on their culture or gender. This is often called *argumentum ad hominem;* that is, leaving the main point in a discourse to attack the person of the speaker. You may have heard people say, "That is how people from his or her part of the country reason/behave".

It is a clear deviation from the main point of discourse to descend into the tactic of attacking the messenger and not addressing the message. In the process of dialogue, evaluation is not altogether negative if it is restricted to what is being said, but this should be done after the speaker has finished making his or her point. There is need to resist engaging in evaluation until you fully understand the speaker's point of view. To do this, it is important to: give everyone the benefit of the doubt by assuming that the speaker is a person of goodwill; ask for clarifications; distinguish facts from inferences; differentiate between opinions and personal interpretations by the speaker; and identify biases or prejudices that may lead the speaker to slant information unfairly.

Responding is the end of a phase of listening process, which then opens the door into another phase. This could be in two stages. The first stage is called a supportive response, which is done while the speaker is speaking. You give a supportive response by saying things like: "I see", "Really", "Is that so?" All these go a long way to show you are actively listening to the speaker and that you are urging him or her on to continue whatever is being said. On the contrary, a response can be summative, in which case it is given at the end of the speaker's speech. This is the stage at which you ask for clarification, challenge the point made, or agree with it.

Responding in the communication process is what was referred to as homeostasis in the Systems Theory, as described in the second chapter of this book. It is response in the form of feedback that keeps the flow of communication going. In this process, there is an exchange of roles. The initiator of the dialogue is the sender in the first instance, while the person to whom the message is directed is the receiver. However, when a response is given, the receiver internalizes the message and gives feedback; at this point, the one who was hitherto the sender in the process becomes the receiver, after having digested the given message. Responding is only made possible if one is able to listen and perceive both the verbal and non-verbal aspects of communication in a dialogue.

Increasing Listening Effectiveness

After having examined the different phases of listening and their importance to the process of dialogue, the next question one can ask is: How can listening effectiveness be increased in all phases so that a better dialogue experience can be achieved? Although there are many ways to have a more effective listening process, we shall look at this from the following angles:

Empathic and Objective Listening: To be empathic is to put one's self in the shoes of another person. This is difficult, since no one can really fill the shoes of another person. It is often said only the one who wears the shoes knows where they pinch. This is what happens in a situation of bereavement or any other mishap, and people say, "I know how you feel", and some retort by saying, "No you do not!" At any rate, what is said about empathy here is to do unto others as you would have them do unto you. It is way of feeling like others.

Objectivity requires removing all forms of bias or prejudices so as to see things as they really are without any form of coloration.

As such, this is the act of feeling with the speaker and seeing the world as he or she does. Sometimes, however, it may be necessary to put your empathic responses aside and listen in a more detached and analytical way. In this way, objectivity is emphasized. To encourage empathy and objectivity, one must try to eliminate any physical or psychological barriers in the listening process.

Nonjudgmental and Critical Listening: This is more or less like objective listening since one is called to listen with an open mind, and then evaluate the message. It goes beyond objective listening because it introduces the aspect of critical listening. This simply means to be aware of your personal prejudices, like religious or ethnic biases, so as not to distort your message or give undue importance to something because it favors you. As we have noted above, no one comes to a dialogue process without some form of bias. The fact that we may come from different parts of the world, speak in a certain way, worship God in a distinct way, or have some level of education shows that we necessarily have certain things which differentiate us from others. The crux of the matter is for us to be aware of these differences and how they can enable or hinder our communication with others.

A judgmental listener stands the chance of shutting out the speaker who can feel that whatever he or she says is going to be looked at through the prism of personal prejudice or unnecessary criticism. Suffice to say, criticism itself is not bad if done constructively. You may offer constructive criticism to someone with whom you are dialoguing after having heard the person out – not during the presentation of his or her ideas. In this instance, constructive critical listening shows you are following what is being said and asking for clarification of facts. The speaker will be glad to offer what other information might be needed if he or she sees that the listener is acting in good faith.

Surface and Depth Listening: All communication messages or dialogue have both ordinary and deeper meanings and, to decipher these meanings, you need to engage in depth listening. To do this, one needs to recognize both the consistent and inconsistent "packages" of messages and take these cues as guides to the meaning the speaker is trying to communicate. Recall what happens sometimes when you drive down a highway on a sunny day and you look far ahead. Most often you see what is known as a mirage on the horizon. That is, as you look ahead, you seem to see a pond of water on the road, but as you move closer to that spot you see there is no water.

When you look far into the horizon, it appears that the sky curves and meets with the earth at a certain point. If you happen to get to that spot where the earth appears to join with the sky, you will see the same thing further ahead. This is similar to what happens in the process of dialogue. You have heard something and you think you really understand what has been said, but upon further reflection on what was said, you get a better understanding of the message. Depth listening is thus a second level of signification that gives better comprehension of the message in the process of dialogue.

Active and Inactive Listening: Active listening is a process of putting into some meaningful whole your understanding of the speaker's total message; that is, the verbal and nonverbal, the content and the feelings you experience in the process of dialogue. To be an active listener, you must paraphrase the speaker's meaning, express understanding of the speaker's feelings, and then ask questions if necessary to clarify your understanding. This shows that you are listening, helps you to check how accurately you have understood what has been said, helps you to express acceptance of the speaker's feelings, and assists you in prompting the speaker to further explore his or her feelings and thoughts.

The second aspect of this section, inactive listening, can also be called passive listening. This is the act of being attentive and supportive but less involved, and this could be desirable in certain circumstances. There are moments, especially in a situation of bereavement, when the only thing needed is not to say anything but just be present. A simple pat on the back goes a long way to communicate that one is listening and attentive to the situation, albeit in a passive way. Also, the non-verbal aspect of a simple nod of the head can signify that a process of dialogue is being well followed.

As a sequel to the aforesaid, there are myriads of situations where a failure to listen to others has brought untold hardships to relationships, families, and nations. A clear example is the Arab Spring in early 2010 where, beginning with Tunisia, other nations like Libya, Egypt, Yemen, Syria, and Bahrain toppled what was deemed oppressive governments after those in power refused to listen to the plight of their citizens for many years. The same is true of the #ENDSARS protest which began shortly after the 60th Independent Anniversary of Nigeria in October 2020.

SARS is the acronym for Special Anti-Robbery Squad, a unit of the Nigeria Police. This arm of the police was started in the early 1990s, not by an act of parliament but by the then Inspector General of Police to combat serious crimes in the nation. However, this unit has been bastardized by certain persons within its rank and file. There are alleged cases of physical and sexual assault, extortion, kidnapping, and killing of innocent citizens by officers of this squad. For many years, the citizens called for the government to reform the police and bring culprits to book but those in power refused to listen. As such, the protest that began in the second week of October 2020 was long overdue.

Despite years of promises by the Inspector General of Police, Mohammed Adamu, to reform SARS, in the heat of the 2020 protest, he said to the chagrin of many, that he was going to redeploy officers of the squad to other police units without addressing the wrongs done or bringing culprits to book. He also announced the formation of a new outfit to be known as Special Weapons and Tactics Team (SWAT). Shortly after this announcement, there was media footage of this new group supposedly in training.

Due to the kid-gloves with which the government had handled issues of incessant police brutality and the refusal to listen to the plight of the average Nigerian, the youth have, through the #ENDSARS protest, demanded a total reform not just of the police but also of the system of government that created the brutal police in the first place. For many years, they had decried politicians taking high pay while the majority of Nigerians languish in abject poverty with non-existent necessary amenities. In the #ENDSARS protest, therefore, just as in the Arab Spring, one sees the effects of a government's refusal to listen to its citizens.

In this chapter, we have examined the process of dialogue with a special focus on listening. We have seen how this act may seem simple but is nevertheless complex as it helps to keep the process of dialogue going. Listening is the act which shows how what is shared by the sender in the process of communication is received and understood by the receiver so that the appropriate response is given in the form of feedback. In this chapter, we have also seen that listening is not limited to the verbal aspect of communication, but that a great deal also happens in the non-verbal dimension. The different phases of listening were also examined and the need to increase listening effectiveness was emphasized.

The crux of this chapter is in affirming that we need to begin listening from within each human person in order to better listen to others. A Latin adage says, *"Nemo dat quod non habet";* that is, "No one gives what he/she does not have." To be effective in listening to others, one must begin by listening to oneself. Many quarrels and misunderstandings experienced in families, offices, and among nations of the world can be traced to the inability of participants in the dialogue process to first listen to their own inner thoughts and emotions so that they can be well equipped to listen to others. Consequently, this chapter calls for us all to begin to view listening from a positive dimension, pay more attention to our inner thoughts, and listen more actively to others anytime we are engaged in the process of dialogue.

CHAPTER FOUR

---•---

Influence of Intra-personal Dialogue on Interpersonal Communication

In the beginning was dialogue. Dialogue permeates and shapes every aspect of human life. The thesis of this book is that dialogue, which influences various aspects of life, begins at the intra-personal level of communication. This is demonstrated in the encounter between Mr. James and Mr. John. On a fateful morning, Mr. James gets to the office in a particular firm, sees a colleague of his, Mr. John, and greets him with, "Good morning." To his surprise, Mr. John shouts back, "What is good about this morning?" Mr. James did not take lightly the outburst from Mr. John and asked why he was shouting at him. Mr. John retorted with a louder yell, telling Mr. James to do whatever he deemed fit, if he felt bad about the way he responded to his greeting.

The verbal altercation between these two drew the attention of other colleagues as they gathered to witness the scene, and they either sided with Mr. James or Mr. John. It took the intervention of their supervisor to quell the tension between these two. In response to the supervisor's effort at getting to the bottom of this furor, which had eaten deep into the early working hours in this firm due to the scene that had been created, Mr. John, after a few minutes of being calm, revealed that he had come to work that morning with a feeling of being a failure, having lagged behind on deadlines a couple of times in the past.

Mr. John had come to a point at which he experienced an inner battle each morning when he came to work, as he now felt every colleague put undue pressure on him since, contrary to his own situation, his colleagues apparently completed allocated tasks in good time. As such, nothing was good for him not just about that morning, but about every morning he stepped into the company to begin another day of unmet targets, with the attendant fear of losing his job. He was therefore spurred on to attack any colleague, and Mr. James just happened to be in the line of fire that morning.

In this episode, we see a typical example of how someone's inner dialogue affects not just the person he/she engages in interpersonal communication but also a multitude of persons. One of the great scholars in this field, William Isaacs, holds that: "When you hear a word like dialogue, you probably think of conversations with others. But, strange as it may sound, dialogue begins with yourself. In fact, all great practices always begin with the individual, no matter how many people one eventually touches" (2010: 88).

As propounded by the Systems Theory, which we examined earlier, dialogue that happens within the individual is a product of the person functioning as a system with many aspects involved. A lot of factors affect and influence the dialogue within an individual, and these factors shape how such a person communicates with the outside world. These and other factors are what this section of the book peruses, as we now try to understand what is meant by the term "intra-personal" and how it is used in the context of communication.

Intra-personal Dialogue and Self-concept

Intra-personal dialogue can be understood by dissecting the two words that make up the term, "intra" and "personal". The word "intra" has to do with what is done at an internal level. It is a way of looking inward and, when connected with "personal" and used in the context of communication, it shows the dimension of communication that takes place within the human person. The process of communication begins within the person since each one of us is endowed with the capacity to think, reflect, and have ideas. Human thoughts are processed internally before they are reflected in external actions.

The act of processing this internal message is what is called intra-personal communication. Each of us can think of what happens to us on a daily basis as we deliberate within ourselves. Human beings are always communicating one thing or the other internally. A great percentage of what happens in our interaction with others begins with our intra-personal dialogue. Many factors condition the internal dialogue we engage in daily, and these include: the image we have of ourselves, that is, our self-concept of who we are; our past experiences; gender; and cultural underpinnings. We shall examine each of these, beginning with self-concept.

Self-concept is an aspect of intra-personal communication that deals with the way we view ourselves, that is, our feelings and thoughts about our strengths and weaknesses, abilities and limitations. Our self-concept is a function of our self-image. These two are interrelated and interdependent. If you have a positive self-concept, it will show in the kind of self-image you present to the outside world. We live in a world that prides itself on image making. Many companies will do anything to maintain a good image of themselves on the societal sphere. The same is true of almost every other aspect of life, as even religious organizations, nations, and private individuals are not left behind in the quest for a positive image.

In the world of social media, many persons go to great lengths to present a good image of themselves. People display the best picture of themselves on Facebook, Twitter, and other social media so as to present a good self-concept of themselves to the outside world. If self-concept is vital to self-image, which in turn conditions intra-personal dialogue and its external manifestation in relationships with people, what then can be said to be the source of self-concept? Among the many factors on which scholars agree we develop self-concept, are the following:

The image others have of you: Everyone has someone they refer to consciously or unconsciously as their "significant other". We often look up to these persons for guidance or acceptance. Your significant other may be a role model, parent, spouse, or friend. No matter who this person may be, the fact is that he or she exerts some influence on you, and you would not want to do anything to upset such an individual. Permit me to cite the example of Joyce, a young professional who for many years had been denied a promotion in her place of work. She was diligent in duty and made a great profit for the company. However, when the time came for promotion, she was always bypassed, while younger members of staff were placed above her.

Joyce endured this for many years until the situation became worse in the sense that she began to feel oppressed by those who had been her juniors but had now become her senior colleagues through promotion. Each time she wanted to protest the injustice she was facing at work by pointing this out to her superiors or by resigning from work, she was reminded of how she would be disappointing her family who looked up to her and would now see her as a quitter. Many other persons in our world today are like Joyce; in patient endurance, they accept whatever insult and injustice are meted out to them just because they want to maintain a good image with their significant others. For Joyce, it was her family; for others it could be someone else special in their life whom they do not wish to disappoint.

In contrast with the above story of Joyce, there may have been situations in which the way we are affirmatively viewed by our significant other has helped to shape how we see ourselves in a positive way and thus contributed to efforts we make towards success. As kids, we may have been told by our parents and teachers that we should be good and take our studies seriously, and this injunction may have helped us excel in academics. Personally, each time I took the second or third position in my high-school class of 40 students, I remember getting home and being queried by my mother: "Does the kid who got the first position have two heads?" This was her simple way of saying that I had the same capacity as whoever came first in the class, and as such, I could be the person to take the first position.

As if the nudging I got at home was not enough, my high-school principal, Mr. Bamkefa, was a role model to us, his students. Mr. Bamkefa was the principal of one of the highly rated secondary schools of the time – Fatima College, Ikire. Before the creation of Osun State from the old Oyo State, Fatima College ranked among the first five secondary schools in Oyo State. The list was usually St. Theresa's Minor Seminary, Government College, Loyola College, St. Patrick's Grammar School, and Fatima College. These schools have produced students who excelled in all walks of life. Upon transfer of my parents who worked for Oyo State government from Ibadan to Ikire, since both towns were within the same State back then, Fatima College, being a Catholic school was a school of choice.

Situated on the serene Ako hill, Ikire, Fatima College used to be a boys-only Catholic school, and the vast expanse of land with trees adorning the lawns and well-structured buildings made the school conducive for learning. Gaining admission to this school was highly contested both from within and outside the state. Students from the school excelled not only in academics but also in sports and other extra-curricular activities.

I remember vividly as we used to sing in the school bus when going to or coming back from sporting activities with other secondary schools. We chanted at the top of our voice: "Oh little little Fatima, Oyo State Champion, we are going to conquer, all other champions." We had a school driver, Mr. Adedeji, aka "Old Boy", whose driving prowess took a new dimension each time he heard us sing this song in the school bus. Students of Fatima College at the time of Old Boy as school driver may remember his popular saying, "Paddle your own canoe", each time we reminded him to be careful while driving.

The boarding facility offered by this school was not equalled by most other schools of the time, and in those days, to be a boarder was a thing of prestige. Founder's Day celebration was one of the highlights of school life at Fatima College as we all gathered in the school chapel for Mass and social events after Mass, with a good number of the alumni gracing the occasion. In my final year of high school, I was privileged to be the Chapel Prefect. It was therefore an honor for me, in that capacity, to plan for the Founder's Day Mass and welcome the alumni back to their alma mater in the Chapel. Fatima College was indeed, a high school like no other. As such, the choice of principals for the school was carefully made in order to keep up the school's high standard. This explains why Mr. Bamkefa's choice as our principal came as no surprise.

Mr. Bamkefa was not just a brilliant teacher of chemistry, but he was also the head of the union of principals in the Local Government Area at the time. We longed to see him in his neat and well-pressed white shirt on the assembly ground. Mr. Bamkefa usually came to address us after the Morning Prayer which was led by Rev. Fr. Alphonsus Flatley, SMA, who was the school Chaplain. After the prayers, we usually chanted the School Anthem, "Oh Come to the Throne of Grace". After these rituals, Mr. Bamkefa will emerge in his immaculate white shirt. He always had a mint 10 naira note, together with one blue and one red pen hanging in his shirt pocket.

He was indeed a model for neatness, academic excellence, and moral probity. Each time any student excelled in an inter-school competition of any sort (sports, quiz or debate), we would be sure to hear from our principal his popular dictum: "More grease to your elbow ... More kerosene to your lantern." It got to the point that we did not wait for him to finish the statement. Once he commenced on the assembly ground to say, "More grease to your elbow," the entire school chorused back, "more kerosene to your lantern."

In those days, the supply of electricity was scarce and, sad to say, the situation has not yet improved in Nigeria at the present time. There was always the shout of "Up NEPA!" whenever the National Electric Power Authority, as they were known, supplied electricity. Over the years, this national power supply company has been known by various names including but not limited to Power Holding Corporation of Nigeria (PHCN), Disco, Genco, etc., but with the various changes in name, there has not been a corresponding positive change in power supply. As such, with this condition of electricity in Nigeria, if you wanted to excel as a student, you had to burn the midnight oil as the saying goes.

About this time in Nigeria, there were stories of house fires when students used candles to study at night and fell asleep in the process. As such, the kerosene-powered lantern was the more accepted option. Hence, Mr. Bamkefa encouraged us to "burn more kerosene in our lanterns" while studying in the wee hours of the night. With this simple gesture, our principal taught us that the prize for hard work is more work. We all tried not to disappoint this significant other, and the training we received from him continues to assist us even till the present time.

Worthy of mention also is my English teacher in high school. In my mind at the time, I prided myself as one of the best English students in the school having represented the school, Our Lady of Fatima College, in quiz and debate competitions, and winning some awards along the way. However, there was this English teacher, Mrs. Odewale, whom I was not a fan of because I felt she was not giving me the high grades I expected for an "English scholar" like myself.

Mrs. Odewale later turned out to be one of my best teachers when I was leaving high school since her encouragement enabled me to achieve the highest grade in my high-school final examinations in English language. With the benefit of hindsight, it is obvious how ignorant I was in my junior high school days to have thought she marked down my scripts. Like her, many teachers mean the best for their students but the students do not see it in that light at the time.

In the days of my junior-high school, I did not get good marks from Mrs. Odewale's English tests due to my negligence of not dotting the "i" and crossing the "t". I queried why the teacher was concerned about such trivial matters! She kept reminding me, however, that I could do better, and her persistence earned me the high grade I obtained in the finals. To date, I always remember to dot my "i" and cross the "t", and each time I do, I chuckle, remembering how I arrived at this very long walk of doing the right thing by this language. The same is true of my teacher of Yoruba language, Mr. Kehinde Akinbile, who was meticulous in the way he taught us to speak and write the language. Thanks to these and other great teachers who went the extra mile to bring out the best in their students!

As such, an important way of building our self-concept is the way others see us and push us to excel, even if we fail to see their efforts in the positive light at the time. If you are seen as a success story and that you only need to put in more effort, you will begin to act as such, but if you are told you can never do anything right, one way or another, this affects the way you see yourself.

The comparison you draw between yourself and others, that is, social comparison: Society compels certain ways on people with regards to how they see themselves. This societal expectation has led some people to either make the right or wrong choices in life. Consider the example of someone who owns a vehicle on lease and sees his or her neighbor with a brand new car. In order to fulfill whatever he/she considers social expectation, he/she quickly opts out of the lease in order to get a new vehicle even when he/she is not able to foot the bills. The economic downturn that gripped the entire world in 2008 has been linked to this greed of a few persons who have shown themselves to be insatiable with whatever they possess and always compare their possessions with those of others.

This craze for social comparison is fueled by many factors in the developing parts of the world, especially in Nigeria. Here, there is an upsurge of "spiritual shops", where people are not encouraged about the dignity of labor but in which many pastors, in a bid to outdo the other in a claim to miracles, lure unsuspecting adherents and lead them on the dangerous precipice of detrimental comparison between themselves and others. The opulent lifestyle of some of these so-called men of God also creates false hope in their followers, who will do anything to fulfill the "prophecy" of the man of God on their lives. As such, many young persons have taken to Internet fraud, daylight robbery, and other forms of crimes in order to live up to the comparisons they have made.

People also make comparisons between themselves and others in a positive way. A student who feels challenged by his or her peers who excel in examinations and gets more serious with his or her studies is making a good comparison. This was the case I cited above when each time I got home with any position other than the first or second position, I was simply told I could do better. There are also moments when people working in firms and companies engage in healthy competitions to bring out the best in each other. Here, people compare themselves with their colleagues, who may have received awards of excellence due to hard work. Colleagues of such award recipients engage in an inner dialogue that propels them to put more effort into their work and achieve better outcomes so they can be recommended for awards as well.

A great number of innovations in human history can be linked to comparisons people and nations make between themselves and others. There has always been that healthy rivalry among scientists to come out with the latest innovations in the field of medicine. Humanity's exploration into space is an example of how one nation compares itself positively with other nations to bring about development in human society. We see this rivalry in space exploration among Russia, the United States, and China, to mention just a few. A lot of satellite-based innovations we enjoy today are due to the bold steps taken by these nations as they try to outdo one another.

In recent times, the information and technological advancement in our society is made possible because companies compare their products with those of others and strive to be better than their rivals. In all these positive ways of comparing one's self with others, the individual who intends to be better at what he or she does must necessarily begin at the intra-personal level of examining what stage he or she stands in order to know how to better himself or herself. As such, social comparison can be either positive or negative, but both of these attitudes begin from the inner chambers of an individual.

Cultural experiences in terms of race and gender: Culture is said to be the toolkit containing everything about an individual. It reveals not just everything about a person's present situation but also past experiences and future aspirations. To better understand the human person, there is need to examine the cultural under-pinnings which shape and guide what the person does. Although some persons may display a higher degree of cultural affiliation than others, suffice to say, there is no one in the world who is not influenced by the culture within which he or she was brought up. Sociologist John Dewey is believed to have said that a child cannot be socialized outside of the society within which he or she grew up. Hence, the way we talk, dress, eat, and even the ethos we observe, are all based on the culture that forms us.

Culture, despite being of immense value to the human person, also imposes some dichotomy or distinctions on us in terms of race and gender; differences which, if overstretched, may be det-rimental to human relationships. The distinctions create certain roles that persons who belong to a certain race or gender are expected to play. Sometimes these roles are unwritten codes, since people just assume that is what is expected of them based on cul-tural norms. Due to these cultural expectations, people engage in inner dialogue as to what to do or not to do owing to cultural impositions on their race or gender.

Consequently, starting with race, this has been on the front burner in recent times. Protest marches have been organized in many parts of the world due to how people of certain races believe they have been unjustly treated by others who consider themselves to be of a superior race. There have been times when traveling has become a very big task for people due to the harrowing experiences such persons are made to go through at the points of entry of certain nations. Racial profiling continues to be a major bane in many Western nations and brutality at the hands of law enforcement agents on account of race is on the increase.

This creates an inferiority complex or the need for people who feel their human rights are trampled upon, on account of race, to assert and defend themselves. Racial profiling creates a thinking process where those who feel marginalized engage in serious intra-personal dialogue to weigh different options before they do anything. I met an African-American lady in one of the parishes where I worked as a supply priest in the United States around 2006. I still remember vividly this woman telling me how challenging it was for people of her race to live in a place they had considered home for many years. She said people had been arrested by law enforcement agents only to later find out they were not even at the scene of the crime for which they were being falsely arrested.

According to this woman, every grocery or other receipts must be well preserved to provide an alibi in case of a wrong arrest and the need to prove where you actually were at the time in question. She said that as African Americans drive down the street, they are constantly in the process of dialogue within themselves about what could happen at the very next block and what they would say in their defense in case of any eventuality. A case in point is that of Ahmaud Arbery, the 25-year-old jogger who was gunned down in broad daylight on February 23, 2020 along Satilla Drive in Glynn County, Georgia, USA. The case was said to have been closed until, due to public outcry, the video footage of the killing was made public and the suspects were arrested, many weeks after the incident.

The same is true of George Floyd, a 46-year-old Black American whose death on May 25, 2020 sparked world-wide protest and the call for equal treatment of persons under the law. The video of

Minneapolis police officer, Derek Chauvin, kneeling on George's neck for almost 9 minutes while the latter was repeatedly saying, "I can't breathe", was gory to watch. Politicians, heads of corporations, and citizens all over the world knelt down in the weeks following this ugly event to signify their disapproval of the act and call for justice for the perpetrators. It took several weeks of protest all over the world before the other three officers involved in the event that led to the death of George were charged.

Barely three weeks after the killing of George Floyd, another African-American man, Rayshard Brooks, was shot and killed by an Atlanta police officer on June 14, 2020. The police was called because Rayshard was said to have slept in his car while driving through a fast-food restaurant. The fracas that ensued when he was to be arrested led to the police shooting him in the back while he was fleeing the scene. There was another ugly event on August 24, 2020 when another unarmed Black man, 29-year-old Jacob Blake, was shot multiple times in the back by the police in Kenosha, Wisconsin, USA. Although the police were said to have been called on account of a domestic dispute, the use of excessive force that resulted in shooting Jacob Blake in the back as he leaned into his SUV while his three children sat in the same vehicle is inexplicable.

The litany of police brutality is quite long, and at the time of writing this book, more ugly occurrences of police harshness are being recorded across the globe. This calls for a re-examination of police strategy in handling situations. In the midst of this, some persons have called for defunding police departments in the United States. Suffice to say, the misconduct of a few police officers should in no way diminish the great sacrifice many upright police officers make to maintain law and order, and everything should be done to support their work. However, it is important to root out bad eggs from the police rank and file.

The situation of maltreatment on account of race has also been reported by many Indigenous people in Canada, despite many years of signing treaties and reconciliation efforts. In the wake of a renewed call for more accountability by the Royal Canadian Mounted Police, Canadian Prime Minister Justin Trudeau affirmed systemic racism exists in the ranks of Canadian police even after RCMP Commissioner Lucki was quoted as saying she struggles with the term. Granted that Canada promotes multiculturalism in various spheres, the protests witnessed in Canada show there is still more to be done. Sometimes, it is the one who feels it who knows it. The ability to listen to others is a great step toward solving problems and eradicating societal ills.

The same issue of maltreatment on account of race is true of persons of Chinese origin because of racial profiling in the wake of COVID-19, which began in Wuhan, China, towards the end of 2019, but has wreaked untold havoc on the entire world throughout 2020. Due to this pandemic, Chinese nationals reported both verbal and physical racial attacks. Many have blamed the Chinese government on account of how the pandemic was handled and their lack of transparency in letting the rest of the world know how serious it was at the outset. However, taking it out on an average Chinese citizen amounts to "cutting off the nose to spite the face."

While it may not be fair to over-generalize these experiences of racial discrimination across the globe, it is also not right to overlook the fact that race plays a great role in the way people relate to one another. Those who belong to a race considered to be inferior will always engage in an inner dialogue that conditions their self-image and is reflected in their outward relationships with others. To this end, many psychologists (Allport, Forbes, Tajfel, Turner) believe stereotyping and prejudice are both cognitive and emotive components of the human person and express themselves in concrete actions of discrimination.

Simply put, prejudice is the distinction we make about other persons because they belong to another group that we consider to be the *outgroup* when compared with ours - the *ingroup*. When those we consider to belong to an *outgroup* do something exceptional, those who belong to the *ingroup* explain it away as being a fluke, but if the same is done by members of our *ingroup*, we celebrate it to the heavens. One of the many ways psychologists believe we can avoid prejudice is through recategorization, by which we shift the boundary between "us" versus "them", so that "individuals who belong to different social groups come to view themselves as members of a single social entity" (Baron & Branscombe, 2014: 226).

Just like race, issues around gender have received more attention in recent times. In the past, the dichotomy between the male and female genders has not only resulted in the downplay of the latter gender, but it has also created inequality in many spheres of life. There have been renewed calls for an appreciation of both genders with equal pay for equal work. In the field of sports, corporate business, and other aspects of life, the call has been the same: Respect each gender as complementary to each other. Despite this call on the international level, many cultures, even in present times, regard females to be inferior to their male counterparts.

As such, in some traditional societies, certain roles are reserved for males, while females are frowned on if they venture into such turf. While not oblivious to the differences in our body makeup, the call has been for an appreciation of each other and the need for one gender not to look down on the other. In some African societies, girl-child education continues to suffer since these male-dominated societies are of the view that "the place of the woman is in the kitchen". Some ethnic groups in Nigeria, for example, marry off their daughters at a very young age since they erroneously believe that, no matter the level of education a woman attains, she will end up in the kitchen; hence, why waste money educating her? This is not only anachronistic but also inhuman to say the least.

Another example of this dangerous dichotomy can be seen in the display of emotions, in which male folk are always told to be strong and tasked to maintain the indifference of the stoic in times of adversity. In Africa, if a male person wants to show emotion in the face of a bad situation, he is quickly reminded to stop "behaving like a woman". Consciously or unconsciously, this becomes the rule of life for male folk. It guides their thought processes, and it conditions the image they have of themselves. On the contrary, any female who tends to exhibit toughness and resilience in any situation of life is quickly told to stop being a "tomboy".

These classifications according to gender and what cultures expect of either the male or their female counterpart have rendered some male folks non-empathetic, since display of emotion is frowned on, and it has also killed the dreams of many females who dared to venture into those areas set out as the exclusive preserve of males by cultural norms. As such, the way cultures view the roles expected of each of the genders is at the base of our thought processes, the internal dialogue people engage in, and our image of who we are and how we should relate to others in society.

Understanding the Self through the JOHARI Window

The JOHARI Window is another way that scholars use to explain the internal dialogue that guides communication and relationships people have with the outside world. This model was developed by two American psychologists: Joseph Loft (1916-2014) and Harrington Ingham (1914-1995), and its name is coined from the combination of the first names of the inventors. The JOHARI Window is a powerful tool of self-awareness that has been employed in psychological, communication, and many other studies to explain how the human person can better understand himself or herself in a bid to relate better with others.

The JOHARI Window is said to be a special tool, which "provides us the opportunity to look into how we view ourselves and how others view us. It acts as a model of opening up the different lines of communication with others. It renders a way to show how we become increasingly more open to others as we get to know them and share information about ourselves" (Saxena, 2015: 135). As such, this method has helped many organizations and companies to bring out the best in their employees and in turn increase productivity and profit through better working relationships, which is the end product of the application of the JOHARI Window. This window is made up of four quadrants known as the open self, the hidden self, the blind self, and the unknown self. This will now be further explained below:

JOHARI WINDOW

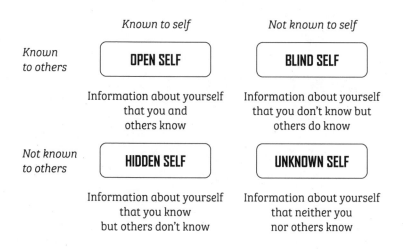

	Known to self	*Not known to self*
Known to others	**OPEN SELF** Information about yourself that you and others know	**BLIND SELF** Information about yourself that you don't know but others do know
Not known to others	**HIDDEN SELF** Information about yourself that you know but others don't know	**UNKNOWN SELF** Information about yourself that neither you nor others know

These are four quadrants with the same size but changes in one quadrant will cause corresponding changes in the others; that is, as one gets bigger, others get smaller. Thus, following Systems Theory, which explains the interconnectedness of entities and which I have set as the theoretical orientation of this book, the quadrants here are parts of a whole that interact with one another and each part is dependent on the other parts.

In preceding chapters of this book, I have also talked about the importance of listening in intra-personal dialogue. Listening is an effective way of increasing self-awareness through the application of the JOHARI Window. That is, listening to others increases the open self as we seek out information to reduce the blind self and become more aware of who we are. Let me now explain each of the quadrants beginning with the open self.

The open self is that part of the quadrant containing information that you know about yourself and others know about you. This is the area in which there is free and open exchange of ideas about you. For example, information about your gender, height, or race are open to the public. The more this quadrant increases, the more people get to know you and the more they better relate with you. What this means is that people are able to tell you more about yourself based on what you allow into the open quadrant. This information leads to better self-awareness, which in turn engenders positive intra-personal dialogue and the effects of this on relationships with others.

The hidden self is that part of you that is known to you alone and that you tend to prevent others from knowing. Many reasons have been given for why people tend to hide certain things from others. This is concerned with the issue of self-disclosure in inter-personal communication. Self-disclosure is a movement from the hidden self to the open self, revealing information about oneself to others. This is influenced by a lot of factors. The first factor here is who you are as a person; that is, are you an extrovert or an introvert? This make-up of the person determines whether you are comfortable or not in being open about yourself.

Culture plays an important role here since certain things are accepted in one culture but not in others. That is, some cultures are more expressive while others tend not to be so. I have earlier talked about gender, but it is also vital here. Certain cultures expect people to be expressive or not based on whether they are women or men. Most African cultures expect the female gender to be more expressive and disclose more than men. One other factor to look at here is the topic of discussion. That is, the more personal and negative a topic may be, the less willing people may be to self-disclose it.

Like any other aspects of life with positive and negative dimensions, scholars hold that there are rewards and dangers to self-disclosure. The rewards include self-knowledge, which brings about a deeper understanding of your own behavior since others are now able to tell you more about yourself. The second reward is communication effectiveness; that is, you understand the message of another person largely to the extent that you understand the person. Dangers of self-disclosure are personal risks, relationship risks, or professional risks. There may be fear of rejection or stigmatization among friends in case of disclosing about a terminal illness, for example. Also, there may be the fear of job loss as a result of a disclosure deemed inappropriate for the job at hand.

To avoid the dangers of self-disclosure, as people struggle through the hidden self towards moving more to the open self, it is good to examine: what motivates one for disclosure; the appropriateness of disclosure at the given time; if others in the communication process are disclosing too; and the burden disclosure might cause. Since dialogue is usually a two-way process, when a person strives to move from the hidden self towards the open self through self-disclosure, certain things are expected of the others to whom one is self-disclosing.

In the context of self-disclosure, the person who decides to share information about himself/herself should be supported by others who should practice active listening, which shows one's empathy towards the speaker by repeating in one's own words what one has heard him or her say. It is also good for the listener to the self-disclosure of another person to avoid making judgments and to keep the disclosure confidential. The movement from the hidden self to the open self is important for self-awareness, but the effort at making this movement is to be made by everyone engaged in the communication process.

The blind self is that quadrant which contains information we do not know about ourselves but which others know. We have mannerisms, carriage, and a way of speaking that we are not aware of, and sometimes it takes someone else to tell us about such attributes. You may have noticed that we get so familiar with our own environment that we are often oblivious to something as minute as even the smell of our room. In the spring of 2000, I was a senior in the major seminary. At the time, I was the Social Prefect of the seminary with the responsibility of not only planning social events but also serving as the liaison between the student body and external bodies wanting to organize any event with the seminary.

The position of the Social Prefect endeared me to other students after having served as the seminary's Master of Ceremony, librarian, and bookshop manager at various times in the previous years. As such, younger seminarians were able to come to me with whatever was bothering them. That was the case of Jude, a freshman at the seminary that year. Jude belonged to one of the dioceses in the eastern part of Nigeria. He was one of the few who came from that part of the country to study in Ss. Peter and Paul, Ibadan, which is situated in the South-Western part of Nigeria and made up largely of students from the old Lagos ecclesiastical province.

Jude came to me one day visibly shaken and worried. When I enquired what the matter was, he said he was afraid he might be in some trouble. I asked what he did, and he said that one of the senior students had called him to say that the way he walks might be interpreted to be prideful and that is not a good sign for someone training to be a priest. The gist of this matter was the fact that Jude had never seen himself walk in one way or the other. I was humbled by his simplicity but also felt sorry for him due to his fears.

The seminary, I reminded him, is a nursery ground where people come to be formed. I told Jude that no one is perfect and that the senior student was only trying to be of help. I told him we never really know ourselves fully, and it takes a friend to tell us some things we may not know about ourselves. The Yorubas in Nigeria have a saying that there is no way we can master the art of walking without one's head shaking while we walk. This is to say, no matter how perfect we think we are, there is always something we need to work on.

However, it takes a good friend to usually reveal to us the part we need to work on. At the same time, the way the blind self is revealed also matters. The Yorubas are a deeply cultural people, and they have great respect for elders. If a Yoruba person notices that an elderly individual has bad breath, the younger person will not just say bluntly, "Sir, your mouth has a foul smell." Rather, the younger person is apt to say, "Please sir, I do not know if you are aware of this particular brand of toothpaste that I heard is very effective; it might be nice for you to try it out." The elder will get the message and do what is needed.

When Jude came to me with his concern, despite the fact that he was not told nicely by the senior student who accosted him, I made him realize we all have something to work on and that he should take the correction in good faith. Today, Jude is a priest and doing well in ministering to God's people. As one can deduce from the case of Jude, the blind self is a delicate part of the quadrant, which, if not well handled, can lead to problems between communicating parties. Two things needed here are the ability to offer constructive criticism and the necessity of accepting correction so as to remove blindness and get to know oneself better.

The fourth quadrant is the unknown self, which confirms the notion that the human person is a complex being. The complexity of the human person shows that we cannot really fully understand humans. The person you think you know today may begin to exhibit certain attitudes that you never deemed possible. In the last 20 years, I have had the privilege of journeying with many people on marriage and relationship issues in which one of the spouses has claimed that, with what is happening in their relationship, it appears they had been married to a stranger all along. This was the case of Mike and Mary earlier mentioned in chapter one of this book.

If the issues surrounding breakdowns in relationships are stretched further, sometimes the one who causes the breakup later says he or she did not know why she or he acted the way she or he did. Even among ordinary friends, you may have observed some kind of behavior that was hitherto never noticed in your friend. If you seek an explanation, you may be told none can be given. All of these show that people cannot really say they know themselves fully. As such, this aspect of the quadrant deals with those features of the human person that are neither known to the person nor to any other.

Apart from the examples given above, there have also been occasions where people engage in certain acts that they never believed they could accomplish. Certain early childhood issues are usually not known by individuals unless otherwise informed by parents, and no one knows when his or her life will end. The unknown issues in this quadrant include "capabilities, feelings, attitudes, aptitudes, which can be positive and useful, or they can be of profound depth in analyzing the deeper aspects of a person's personality; influencing his/her behavior to various degrees" (Saxena, 2015: 138).

The way to reduce the unknown self quadrant is to reduce both the hidden and blind self so that the open self may increase. That is, reduce the hidden self by revealing more information about yourself and accept what is said about you by others in the blind self, especially when it is constructive criticism. Once these other two quadrants decrease, and the open self increases, the person gets to know more about himself or herself and thereby reduces the unknown self.

In essence, the JOHARI Window is an effective way of analyzing the notion of self-concept, which is an important ingredient in intra-personal dialogue. The way we see ourselves conditions the kind of attitude we have towards people around us and the relationships we build with them. People who have been told they are success stories have built their image around that narrative, and most times they have succeeded in life. On the other hand, those who feel they are nothing but a failure exhibit the same negative attitude in everything they do, thereby fulfilling the prophecy of being a non-achiever.

Employing the JOHARI Window through the open, blind, hidden, and unknown Self, we have shown here how the human person is both complex and interconnected, not just with others but also with every experience of life. When you relate with people, it is important not just to focus on what is being said at a given time, but also to be conscious of the fact that each individual's engagement in external communication is guided by his/

her intra-personal dialogue. This is, in turn, a function of his/her self-image and other experiences of life. While the four quadrants examined here are vital to understanding self-concept, the need to decrease the other three quadrants while enlarging the open self is a way to better know the individual and bring about an effective process of dialogue.

The Samaritan Woman's Encounter with Jesus: A Practical Application of JOHARI Window

In the Christian faith, the Bible is not just a compendium of many great books, but it is at the same time the Word of God. This Word has many stories for edification, correction, and encouragement of the faithful (2 Tim. 3:16). One of the biblical stories that speaks to the issue of dialogue, movement from the unknown to the open self, and the effects of these on the lives of not just those engaged in communication but also of entire communities is the story of Jesus and the Samaritan woman (John 4:5-42). Using the symbolism of water and thirst, Jesus took this woman to a higher level of signification and fulfilled her innermost thirst.

St. Augustine said, "Our hearts are restless until they rest in God." This can be said of this woman based on the communication and dialogical way with which Jesus satisfied her inner longing. The document of the Catholic Church on Social Communication, *Communio et Progressio*, no. 11, presents Jesus as the perfect communicator, since: "He adjusted to His people's way of talking and to their patterns of thought." Hence, Jesus knows the best way to dialogue with people and, using simple symbols, bring them to a high level of understanding of their own situation without imposing his own position on them.

This was the case in the episode in the fourth chapter of John's Gospel where Jesus is presented as the one in need. He was tired out from his journey, probably thirsty for water, and maybe in need of food since his disciples had gone into the city to buy food. He saw someone who was thirstier than himself in the woman who came to draw water from the Well of Jacob. In life, we thirst for many things other than water. When sick, we thirst for good health. Good health is what the entire world thirsts for at the time of writing this book when the COVID-19 pandemic is ravaging the globe. This has had devastating effects with an unprecedented number of deaths and sick people, warranting the shutdown of the entire world – schools, offices, churches, and travels.

The stay-at-home order has compelled humanity to satisfy the long-ignored thirst of being there for one another as members of the same household since we live in a very fast-paced world. In the midst of the pandemic, we were made to slow down, take a pause, and examine issues of relationships between humans – and for people of faith, to take deeper look at our relationship with God. Although there were many conspiracy theories about the pandemic, the fact remains that it has brought about a "new normal" to human existence. The devastation and death caused by COVID-19 is unprecedented.

At the beginning of the summer of 2020, when many nations were trying to open up in phases, there had been 4,315,679 persons infected with the virus worldwide. Out of this, there were 294,879 deaths in the United States and a total of 74,540 infected persons with 5,553 deaths and 36,760 recoveries in Canada. In Nigeria, there were 5,162 infected persons, 167 deaths, and 1,180 recoveries. By the end of June 2020, when many persons in the Western hemisphere expected to enjoy festivities in the summer months, there had been more than half a million COVID-19 fatalities globally. As the summer festivities were winding down by the end of

August 2020, there were more than 25 million cases of COVID-19 globally. These figures keep rising by the day.

As the plague lingers on, the entire world thirsts for an end to this pandemic. Respite came the way of humanity when on November 9, 2020, after many months of research by many pharmaceutical companies all over the world, Dr. Albert Bourla, Pfizer Chairman and CEO announced that it was a great day for science and humanity since the first set of results from the third phase of the COVID-19 vaccine trials yielded positive ways of combating the pandemic. This was a piece of news for which the entire world had thirsted for many months.

A week after the news of a vaccine by Pfizer and Bion-tech, another biotechnological company, Moderna Inc. announced another COVID-19 vaccine, which was considered a development on the one earlier announced since it does not require extreme cold temperatures for storage like the one by Pfizer/Bion-tech. Following these two companies, many other pharmaceutical companies have come up with vaccines and the list keeps increasing. The world heaved a sigh of relieve when on December 8, 2020, the first doses of the Pfizer vaccine were given to people in the United Kingdom. The Pfizer vaccine arrived in Canada on December 13, 2020. Many other nations have followed suit as each tries to satisfy the thirst of citizens for good health.

We also thirst for justice when we feel wronged. Examples abound in George Floyd, Rayshard Brooks, and the American jogger, Ahmaud Arbery, who was shot in his prime in Georgia, United States. These and similar cases call for justice from various quarters. We thirst for progress at work and peace in our homes. In the face of the lockdown on account of COVID-19, which brought the world to its knees for a couple of months in the beginning of 2020, the thirst for some persons was just to go out and have a haircut! The list of human thirsts is inexhaustible. The woman at the Well of Jacob had a thirst that was more than what water could satisfy. We shall get to know more about this woman's thirst later in her dialogue with Jesus.

As he always does with us who believe, it was Jesus who started the dialogue with the Samaritan woman. He asked her for a drink. As we are prone to do in any given communication process, she was ready to place lots of obstacles to distort this dialogue that Jesus initiated. She started by asking why Jesus, a Jew, would ask her, a Samaritan, for a drink? There is so much to understand about the relationship between the Jews and Samaritans, which had gone sour despite the fact that they were children of the same father – Jacob. In fact, it was at the Well of Jacob that this dialogue took place. In normal circumstances, both Jews and Samaritans should have access to this well. When Jesus broke through the first barrier, the woman was quick to throw in another obstacle when she said that even if she wanted to give Jesus a drink, he had no bucket.

Jesus saw beyond these barriers the woman was trying to place as the clog in the wheel of the dialogue he was having with her. He persisted and told her that if only she knew who it was who asked her for water, she would have been the one to ask him for living water. It was at this point in the dialogue that Jesus struck a chord of resonance in this woman. She was thirsty about many things, and it was a great relief to hear that someone was able to satisfy her thirst.

It is important for us to note some of the things this woman was thirsty about. In the first place, she went to fetch water alone and at noon! This was strange among the Jews. At the time in question, women went to the well as a group and mostly in the early hours of the morning. The question then is: Why did this woman go alone and at noon, under the heat of the midday mid-eastern sun?

The answer can be found in the dialogue that ensued between the woman and Jesus, after he promised to give her living water, for which she would never be thirsty again. Jesus asked the woman to go and call her husband, and she responded that she had none, despite the fact that she was living with a man at that time. This was the point in the dialogue when there was a movement from the unknown to the open quadrant for this woman. Jesus revealed a very deep secret that was not even known to the woman concerning her current marriage. He told her although she had been married five times, even the man she was living with at the time was not her husband (Jn. 4:18). It was at this point the woman began to wonder what kind of man Jesus was, who had revealed to her things about her past and present life.

At that moment, what began with the simple request for water took on a deeper and more important dimension. It revealed why the woman was alone at the well at noon. At the time of Jesus, people frowned on adultery as contained in the Law of Moses (Leviticus 20:10). As such, a woman who had had five husbands was not looked kindly upon by the community of the time. This explains why the other women in the village would not have anything to do with her or allow her to join them while going to the well in the early hours of the day. The Bible did not tell us about these five husbands until Jesus mentioned them, or why they left the woman (it was uncommon for a woman to divorce a man at that time). As such, it was a situation that brought about social seclusion and agony in that woman.

When Jesus took her through the journey of the unknown to the open self, she could not contain her joy as she ran to the village, to the same people who had earlier ostracized her, to tell them about this "man" who told her everything she ever did. After the villagers encountered Jesus, the story concluded with the villagers saying to the woman: "We no longer believe just because of what you said; now we have heard for ourselves, and we know that this man is the saviour of the world" (Jn. 4:42). Each of the villagers came to a better understanding of their peculiar situation because of the presence of Jesus in their village. In essence, dialogue often begins small, but it always has several dimensions if allowed to flourish.

In this story, the conversation around the issue of water later developed and metamorphosed into something that helped the woman to know herself better, and there was also the community dimension since the entire village now believed in Jesus. Have you ever considered any dialogue to which you are invited as something trivial? The example of the dialogue between Jesus and the woman at the Well of Jacob should make you understand why you need to change this view. When we dialogue, so many things happen that we get to know more about ourselves or the situation at hand as the discussion opens more vistas, which move us from the blind, hidden, or unknown self to the open self.

As you read this book, you will acknowledge that no day passes without you having some inner dialogue within yourself. Think of those inner conversations concerning your job, a relationship, or some decision you had to make on an important aspect of your life. Sometimes, you do this without actually acknowledging what you are doing. While some of these inner conversations occur within split seconds, some others keep you awake all night. Some are choices you make between issues that are as distinct and clear as the difference between night and day, while others are very complex situations whereby choices are similar and confusing. Some of these inner conversations are easy to share with others, while some are weights you have to bear alone.

A great many of these inner dialogues might be easily resolved, while some may take months or years to resolve. Some of these inner conversations are obscure, while some others are eye opening as they reveal more about ourselves or others. The point remains that no day passes without each and every one of us engaging in this inner dialogue and, even when they seem simple, the consequences of such inner deliberations are sometimes great when they are manifested externally. If we are blessed to see someone who is able to assist us in giving form to our inner dialogue, like the Samaritan woman who saw Jesus, then the weight of that inner dialogue becomes lighter.

The need to take cognizance of our inner conversation and its external manifestation is required in our world today more than ever before. After the global economic downturn of 2008, many persons lost their jobs, their homes, and even their lives. Depression set in as people could not handle the inner dialogue they were having within them. The same situation is around us with the COVID-19 pandemic. As nations began to gradually open up in phases after months of lockdown, humanity returned to what has been termed the "new normal". This is so, as things we hitherto took for granted – the ability to freely travel from place to place, dinner in restaurants, going to theatres or places of worship – have all been affected by the "new normal".

In light of the COVID-19 pandemic, many jobs were lost while the financial market witnessed the worst downturn in a single day in the month of May, which had not been seen in many decades. Many persons who consider places of worship to be arenas for resolving deep-seated inner battles felt disappointed since even those places were affected by the lockdown. The result of this inner dialogue of fear of the unknown was seen externally through panic-buying of even things people did not need. The fear was palpable in the land as people did not know how long the pandemic would last. For people of faith, it is at such a moment when human ingenuity and capacity fail that another inner dialogue comes to the fore. That is Prayer. In the dialogue of prayer, many not only find solace for their inner battles, they also see a way forward in the midst of challenges.

In the foregoing, I have been concerned with underlining the fact that every human person has inner dialogue, which conditions and shapes our external relationships. Sometimes, these inner dialogues cross our minds in ordinary everyday life events, and we take no notice of them, but they are always there. These inner thoughts can be compared to the oxygen we breathe in without seeing it or even taking cognizance of it, but without it, no one lives.

As you read this book, there are millions of thoughts going through your mind. These thoughts could range from very salient life decisions to trivial matters. You may be thinking of how to pay your mortgage or the topping you want on your pizza. The mind plays its own tricks on us most of the time, when our inner dialogues distract us from very important issues where we should put maximum concentration. Have you ever seen yourself at a meeting, in a place of worship, or in a classroom and your mind is hundreds of miles away? This happens to us all, and it takes a special effort to redirect our inner dialogue back to where it should be.

In sum, this chapter highlights the fact that our inner dialogues do not just happen on their own since they are influenced by our past experiences, self-concept, and many other factors. I also showed, using the JOHARI Window, how we get to better understand ourselves by moving from the hidden, blind, and unknown to the open self. This was concretized in the narrative between Jesus and the Samaritan woman at the Well of Jacob.

The thrust of this chapter is to emphasize the fact that inner dialogue is an inescapable fact of life, and this aspect conditions and shapes the kind of interpersonal dialogue and relationship we have with people. Hence, there is need to take cognizance of this very important aspect of human life. The next chapter of this book examines how human interactions and relationships are being shaped by the new means of communication and what has become of dialogue in this new media and digital age.

CHAPTER FIVE

———————•———————

Dialogue in a Digital Age: Prospects and Challenges

The digital means of communication has become a kind of parliament in the modern age. This is because the digital means of social communication is the *areopagus* within which ideas are discussed and the platform that highlights and directs public opinion. The digital media has made the world go from being called a small village to becoming a desktop since information is now shared across the globe at the click of the mouse. The digital media is dominated by visuals like never before.

One television station in Europe has an advertisement caption that says, "No Comment TV." This displays myriad pictures while muting the audio of the visuals. By this act, people are made to discern the meanings behind these pictures. We live in a world where a single picture speaks a thousand words. Although pictures are used to pass information and ideas from one person to the other, for the sake of clarity in communication, the spoken word has primacy. It is often said that the human language is one of the greatest inventions in history.

Oftentimes, a picture can be interpreted differently by different people. On the contrary, a spoken word, if misunderstood, can be easily elaborated upon for clarity's sake. Many problems in families, corporations, and establishments stem from the wrong use of visuals. Visuals have found a fertile ground in the new media where pictures are used in the forms of emoji instead of a text message. The main concern is that these emoji can be easily misinterpreted by individuals. Apart from the problems associated with visuals, the over-reliance on the new media is creating what Nixon (2012) referred to as the digital tipping point.

The digital tipping point is a situation where people depend so much on digital gadgets that they become estranged from connections with people in close proximity to them. Many young persons today spend a great deal of time glued to their cell phone screens even at road intersections, resulting sometimes in accidents. The disconnect between people has become unprecedented in recent times because of the dependence on digital formats.

To this end, Nixon holds, "Our growing Internet use is diminishing our ability to pay attention, connect disparate pieces of information to form a coherent understanding, and interact with others to negotiate, resolve problems, and create new solutions to the new problems we are facing in our interconnected and overburdened world" (2012: 46). As such, either through over-use of digital form or wrong use of visuals, dialogue continues to elude us in this digital age.

There is the story of a certain pharmaceutical company, which prided itself on having made a great discovery in medicine with regards to a particular ailment. This can be likened to what happened for the greater part of 2020 when there was a race for the COVID-19 therapeutic, and there were claims from various parts of the world that the cure had been found. As pharmaceutical companies in North American and Europe were working to provide a cure for the pandemic, there were news of a cure being found in Madagascar and Nigeria. Some of these claims are yet to be subjected to scientific scrutiny to ascertain their veracity. What is certain is at the end of 2020, there was the provision of the vaccine by Pfizer/Bion-Tech and Moderna to some parts of the Western Hemisphere.

Continuing on the significance of audio-visual aid in communication, the story of the pharmaceutical company that claimed to have made a medical discovery in curing an ailment continues with the assertion that with their innovation, the ailment which hitherto took years to cure can now be treated within days. They were so over-joyed with their effort that they decided to market their product all over the world.

One of the representatives was sent to a particular Arab country where the people gathered in an auditorium to hear about this medical miracle. Since this agent did not understand the language of the people, he decided to communicate with them using pictures. To drive home his message quickly, he put three pictures in a single slide. Reading the pictures from left to the right, the first shows a man who was lying sick on the bed, the next shows the same man taking their patented pill, and the third picture on the extreme right hand, shows the man standing up healthy. As this agent took a bow to signify he had finished his presentation, grinning from ear-to-ear and broad smiles on his proud face, people in the auditorium started throwing bottles and anything they could find at him.

Scampering to safety at the back of the auditorium, he gestured from afar to the man who had earlier introduced him to the audience and enquired why there was this kind of reaction from the people when he had only shown them how his company's product could help them. To his amazement, the other person told him the people understood his product to be deadly. This is because his picture showed a healthy man who takes his pills and then finds himself lying sick on the bed. This misunderstanding stems from the fact that the people in that country read from the right to the left, whereas his picture was explaining something from the left to the right. As such, a picture can convey meaning, but a clearer meaning, one void of ambiguity, is better conveyed through the spoken word.

It is interesting to see how the present civilization has moved beyond just visuals or audio to combine the two in audio-visual means, powered and engineered by present social media. It is also interesting to note that a great deal happens with the combination of audio-visuals in the sense that light, which is the main factor in sight, travels at 186,000 miles per second while sound in the audio aspect travels at 1,100 feet per second. As such, without even noticing it, our senses of sight and hearing do so much work each time we engage in the audio-visual means of communication. The speed accompanying this medium of communication enables news and information to get to anyone around the world at the click of a mouse with utmost immediacy and unprecedented capacity for feedback.

The present digital age has been described by a number of taxonomies. Among others, it has been called the post-modern society, the jet age, the computer age, the Internet age, new media age, etc. In all these, information and communication technology, which form the bedrock of the new media age, continue to shape, define, and refine human existence in every facet of life. The present human civilization, which began with communication in village squares through town criers and messages being transported from one point to another on horseback, has been replaced with the present day online tweeting bird known as the twitter, among others.

One of the effects of this is that the monopoly of knowledge associated with the form of communication that hitherto held sway has been replaced by a kind of free market situation where people acquire knowledge and information at the click of a mouse through their personal computer, blog, Facebook, chat room, LinkedIn, Tumblr, to mention but a few. The impact of this on human civilization can only be imagined as almost everything in the present age is now measured in terms of its media-compliance or otherwise. The analogue equipment that was considered top-notch in years previous has given way to digital counterparts.

Back in earlier days, the radio was defined among the Yorubas of Nigeria as: *"Asoro ma gbesi."* That is, that which only speaks without getting feedback. Not only has the radio gone beyond such understanding, but the Internet has come to make communication immediate and reciprocal. Many radio presenters now use social media like Facebook and Instagram to reach a wider audience.

The new digital means of communication is continuously being developed upon, with effects on many spheres of life. In the face of the modern means of communication, therefore, the question one can ask is: "What has become of dialogue"? How has the new means of communication in this hyper-technological age advanced or stiffened real and engaging dialogue? In what way can we say the media is really dialogical and democratic in our present dispensation?

Dialogical Media and Democratic Participation

It is suffice to reiterate that communication creates and main-tains the unique social and cultural habitat that is the source of individual and collective identity. Despite the prominence given to the new means of communication, it is important to note that the primal form of human communication is human language. Language is a vehicle of expression and, through conversation, people search for identity, sustainability of communities, essence of democratic arrangement, and the requirements of ethical decision-making (Hamelink, 2004: 25).

Within the same human society, as people share the same language and other symbols of communication, some persons often try to suppress or influence others, and the media becomes a ready tool to achieve this aim. In fact, Thomas Hobbes earlier postulated that man is woe unto man. Each one tends to promote his/her personal view, which, most of the time, fails to take others into cognizance. This raises pertinent questions about the dialogical nature of the means of communication. Whether the means of communication is dialogical or not can be traced to the history of persons who engage such media.

Human persons are a composite of many experiences that shape their outlook and worldview. For instance, the experience of colonization and the military dictatorship that followed in many African countries and other parts of the world continues to cast a dark patch on the idea of a democratic modern means of communication. For example, before the advent of the present democratic dispensation in Nigeria, the nation's suffering under the heavy yoke of military dictatorship for many years left lots of implications on many fronts.

During this era, for instance, media was not only subjugated under the heavy hammers of the despots, media professionals were also harassed, unjustly imprisoned, and even wantonly executed. This made some persons in the media profession follow the dictum, "If you cannot beat them, join them." The coming of democratic rule in 1999 was then seen as a panacea to the many years of military junta, which produced a militarized people.

One of the gains of the present democratic dispensation is freedom of expression exemplified in the influx of the modern means of communication starting with the cellular telephone popularly called a "cell phone". The introduction of cell phones gave most people the opportunity to communicate, even though at the early stage of its advent, ownership of phone lines was a luxury as they were sold at exorbitant prices beyond the reach of the ordinary person. I remember the very tedious task I had to undergo to get a mobile phone number when it came to Nigeria in 2001. I had to book for the phone line many weeks in advance, and one was not even guaranteed to get a phone number unless one knew someone in the phone company who was willing to assist. All this came at a very exorbitant price.

The right to communicate and be communicated with, to dialogue in order to share ideas, is an inalienable dimension of the whole gamut of human rights. Suffice to say, different organizations have arisen in human history to clamor for human rights and freedom of expression. Notable among these are the United Nations, non-governmental organizations, and civil liberty organizations, to mention but a few.

With particular reference to freedom of the media, the World Association for Christian Communicators (WACC) was founded in the wake of the 1939-45 World War to oppose the use of propaganda and misinformation in the media. At this time, the media were mainly owned and operated by the government. Since there was no private ownership of media outfits, the government used the media to a large extent as a means of propaganda. As such, WACC gave rise to organizations aimed at making non-aligned countries fight for their liberation from neo-colonial powers and imperialists that dominated their most authentic cultural values.

A democratized and dialogical media, according to many authors, are supposed to strengthen the public domain through the availability of information and knowledge and ensure that access to means of communication is affordable. They should also make certain that people are able to use electronic networks effectively, especially in the development context. Having a dialogical media is supposed to also: secure and extend the global dimension for both broadcast and telecommunication; serve as a watchdog over government and ensure that the government is democratic and transparent; and challenge information surveillance/censorship. Above all, the media are expected to support the community and to be people oriented.

A dialogical understanding of the media is a clear distinction from the view of communication that was hitherto fashionable for a greater part of the twentieth century in which communication, through the linear model, was seen mainly as a one-way act of imposing the view of a few on many others. In the proper perspective, the right to communicate involves freedom and rights of expression, communication privacy, as well as cultural sensitivity in communication (Richstad, 2003: 35).

Building on the foundation laid by WACC, UNESCO has championed the cause of democratizing the media by claiming that the right to communicate is an issue of human rights and should be viewed as a two-way process between partners carrying out a democratic and balanced dialogue. Fisher and Harms broadened this view when they said that:

> Everybody has the right to communicate: the components of this comprehensive Human Right include but are not limited to the following specific communication rights: (a) a right to assemble, a right to discuss, a right to participate

> and related association rights; (b) a right to
> inquire, a right to be informed, a right to inform,
> and related information rights; and (c) a right to
> culture, a right to choose, a right to privacy and
> related development rights (1982: 173).

The rights enumerated here, to a large extent, have been put to use through modern information and communication technology. This has taken communication to a higher echelon as people now share information at the click of a mouse and the erstwhile spatial-temporal barrier to communication continues to be erased. Therefore, with the advent of the Internet in the late 1980s through 1990s, there came an invitation for millions of individuals to communicate. With this advent, a new dimension of human rights to free expression occurred in the history of international communication (Kleinwachter, 1995: 107). It is nevertheless pertinent to note that the over-abundant information available online leads to a corresponding over-dependence on whomever has the means to find and manage the flow of this information.

Growing up in Nigeria in the 1980s, media content was grossly limited as opposed to the super-abundant media programs in place today. At the time, there were three television channels in Oyo State: One was owned by the federal government; the second was owned by the state I lived in; and a neighboring state owned the third television station. Media programs did not begin until 4:00 p.m. and daily broadcasts ended with the network news at 9:00 p.m. It is interesting to see the transformation that has taken place in the same country in the last 30 years with the media-saturated environment that exists at the present time. It is pertinent to note that over-abundance of media products is inversely proportional to how the same product is available to consumers.

Many factors engender over-concentration of media products in the hands of a few. Over-concentration of the means of information in the hands of a few leads to manipulation of others, which may even become an instrument of oppression in the hands of the powerful as seen in the Rwandan genocide of 1994. Here, Radio-TV *Libre des Mille Collines* (RTLM) was alleged to have been used in conducting a persistent campaign against the Tutsis. Rather than being a voice of the people, it became a voice against the people. There is also the example of Kuala Lumpur, Malaysia, where the media were said to be not only supportive of unconditional freedom of information but also for fulfilling human potential to rationally grasp reality and creatively participate in social and cultural life (Nordenstreng, 1984, 30).

In the same Malaysia, women have consistently cried out as being marginalized. Here, development was seen in the notion of tall structures, acquisition of the latest information and communication technology, and deregulation and privatization, which brought about more media outfits but less opportunity for people to air their views (Kim, 2004: 119). The same is true of Thailand where section 39 of the Constitution deals with freedom of expression, but this is not seen in actual practice (Servaes, 2004: 153). The case of many African nations is not far from the aforesaid. Bourgault holds that, "Broadcasting in Black Africa was largely created by the colonial powers, chiefly for their own purposes. And broadcasting on the continent has always been chiefly state-controlled, heavily government-subsidized, and urban-based, usually emanating from capital cities" (1995: 42).

Robert White sees the democratization of communication as a social movement through which marginalized persons or those who do not belong to the mainstream culture find expression for their life situations. For him, this involves the right to access the process of constructing the public cultural truth; the expression of the right to communicate at the institutional, structural, and societal level; participation in administrative and policy decision-making regarding public mass media as the right of the citizen; encouraging a space of cultural dialogue among a broad diversity of interests; a new philosophy of communication and a new normative theory (White, 1995).

White concludes by affirming that, "If democratization of communication is to take place, it is important to become aware of the structural processes, the processes underlying the conditions, and to some extent to be able to seize the moment to create an opening for democratization" (1995: 113). This moment is often described as the educable moment when everyone sees the need for change from the status quo, which does not favor the majority of the people.

A lot of social movements have been able to bring about this change for the good of their society. Apart from seeing social movements as the vehicle for driving democratization of the media, other scholars favor the traditional media to do this. Pradip Thomas (1994) sees traditional forms of communication to be inherently symbolic in content and form since metaphor, metonomy, and the use of discontinuous analogies are some of the means by which symbolic meanings are communicated here.

With special reference to many African societies, traditional forms of communication in the moonlight tales, activities like dancing or wrestling, and rituals like weddings or naming ceremonies are not only democratic and dialogical in nature, but they also invite people to jointly reflect on their stories and chart a way for the future. This has been expressed in an earlier chapter of this book where I talked about the cultural and ethical values of moonlight tales.

It is pertinent to note that "traditional forms of communication (oral media) are becoming not only increasingly subservient to modern communications (mass media and mass communication, telephony, computers, other personal communications services), but modern communication is also getting more abundant and more robust in form" (Ogundimu, 2017: 210). I doubt if children born in the last 10 years have ever experienced moonlight tales. Computer games and the Internet have taken the place of what used to be a traditional medium of dialogue. Many homes now engage their young by putting them in front of the TV set with various kinds of cartoons.

I once had an eye-opening encounter with one of my nephews who was 3 years old at the time. I went to visit his parents, and while we were having a conversation in the living room, I noticed that he was busy operating the television, changing from one channel to the other with a high level of dexterity. When I inquired who had taught him to operate the remote control so effortlessly, the look on his face was priceless. He looked at me as if saying, "Which planet are you from?" After giving me the look, he said, "I just know how to do it." When he said that, my mind went back to when I was 10 years old and the black and white TV we had (which, by the way, had no remote control but sat proudly in our living room on top of a raised platform holding it high up on the wall beyond the reach of us children).

In those days, you needed an adult who was tall enough to reach up to the TV in order to operate it and change channels for you. Maybe it was the big task of operating a TV, which was well beyond our reach, coupled with the limited programs TV offered back then – most of which did not appeal to children – that made us resort to the more traditional means of communication back in those days. In light of the present dispensation where the ease of modern means of communication has displaced traditional media, there is need for a merger between the two forms of communication such that the good aspects of each will be employed towards the democratization of media in order to fulfill their dialogical role, which is the thesis of this book.

Ogundimu highlights four important ways through which African modes of communication can be relevant in the democratic movement of the twenty-first-century information technology in the political, technological, economic, and cultural aspects. In each of these, dialogue is vital. Ogundimu concludes that, "African media need to become more creative and imaginative when it comes to producing not only entertainment but also reporting and analysis of political, economic, and cultural issues ... Unless this is done, it is doubtful if the media can truly tap into local consciousness and channel the abundant energy of the grassroots into fueling the engine of democratization" (2017: 235).

While supporting the need for synergy of the good aspects of both traditional and new media, it is pertinent to highlight that the times are changing, and that the Internet has come to stay as a means of not only communicating but also shaping every aspect of human life. It has brought about a robust dialogical sense to communication and relationship. The online digital media has created a new space for dialogue in a way never witnessed before (Rose, 2016). Immediacy in feedback, which is presently experienced in the media world, has been made possible through the Internet.

The development of this digital technology could be traced to the late 1940s, when images, texts, and sounds were first converted into binary codes – ones and zeroes. This vastly improved the rate at which information is stored and reproduced. The Internet began with its use as an attack-proof military communications network in the 1960s by the United States Defense Department's Advanced Research Projects Agency (ARPA). The original name was thus, ARPAnet or NET for short. Like a cobweb, the Internet gave rise to myriads of websites which continue to link people and ideas together from different parts of the globe. With its ability to offer both personal and mass communication, it breaks down conventional distinctions among the various older media formats and places communication in the hands of everyone.

On account of many factors, some persons will question whether the Internet has truly placed communication in the hands of everyone. There have been a considerable number of studies done on the relationship of people's income, geographical locale, and Internet use. The distinction in computer use among low-income residents and those in wealthier communities was the main argument in the study by Benton Foundation (1998). It was discovered that students in low-income areas would be less able to participate in the interactive aspects of the new technologies than their wealthier community counterparts. In the same vein, Shaw and Shaw (1999) discovered in their study of the same phenomenon that instead of being creative users of the media, students in low-income areas would tend to depend on the interpretations given by those in the urban centers.

Other scholars believe the use of the Internet by students in rural areas is a function of many factors other than the aforementioned. Thus, an empirical study by Lentz, Straubhaar, LaPastina, Main, and Taylor (2000) suggests other variables like public access points in the form of libraries, schools, and community technology. They believe that, when these become readily available, they will broaden students' minds and help in eliminating the digital divide they are subjected to, on account of their location.

With special reference to the African continent, which has a large proportion of low-income communities and a high cost of maintaining an active online presence, many nations have resolved to engage community radio as a way to get involved in media presentation that reflects the situation of the local people. Community radio operates on a small scale by employing the culture of the local people as the raw material for its programming, while people construct meaning through a system of dialogue based on their day-to-day life in such presentations. Nations in East Africa were pioneers on this development in Africa, while other continents have their unique experiences of community radio.

One of the historical discourses on community radio traces its debut to Canada where the Canadian Radio and Television Commission (CRTC) promoted the prefix "community" as a way of showcasing Canadian culture and identity. Canada, it should be noted, has a robust Indigenous presence. Among the First Nations, the community is supreme. Many reserves have elders who help to maintain stability in their community and teach the young the values of community life and survival in their habitat.

As such, bringing out the involvement of local people in community radio, this Canadian commission "distinguished programming made by non-professionals in the community, and local programming made about the community by paid cable company staff" (Lewis, 2002: 52). The important point here is that through this effort by the local people, such radio presentations have brought great development not only to individual lives but also to the community at large. The main point in all this effort is that change is brought about when people employ dialogue in telling their own story.

A replica of Canadian community radio can be seen in citizen journalism, which has taken root in many African nations presently. This novelty is not without an antecedence of years of suppression and lack of dialogue in many aspects of African society. For many years of her existence as a nation, Nigeria has witnessed one military rule after another. Military rule produced a militarized people where the dictum is to "obey without complaint". Dialogue on national issues was sacrificed on the altar of military decrees.

Although the present democratic rule in Nigeria started in 1999, the nation continues to witness military mentality in different sectors due to a militarized people produced from years of military junta. What this entails is that freedom is not only stifled, but the self-expression that enables people to showcase and develop their potential and engage in national dialogue is also downplayed. In the aspect of communication, freedom has been an illusion from the time of the colonial masters who saw media practitioners as clogs in the wheels of their efforts at perpetually subjugating the local people.

The criticism of the colonial masters by certain newspapers of the time was frowned on by Lord Lugard, who sought every opportunity to repress the press. Sir Frederick John Lugard was a British soldier who later became the Governor-General of Nigeria between 1914 and 1919. In 1917, he was said to have introduced permanent censorship – a law that was meant to repeal the Newspaper Ordinance of 1903. According to this law, not only was censorship of newspapers to be introduced, but also the buildings and equipment of a convicted newspaper would be liable to confiscation.

From the irksome treatment meted out to journalists and communication as a whole in the hands of colonial masters, to the harrowing experience of the civil war in a nascent independent Nigeria in 1960 and the long years of military dictatorship that followed, freedom of expression and democratization of communication continues to elude a people so familiar with oppression and at home with domination. As I said earlier in this book, a respite came at the threshold of the new millennium when the newly established democratic government in 1999 brought about an influx of cell phones to Nigeria. This was accompanied by the nation's debut into cyberspace with the launch of Nigeria-Sat 1 and other cyberspace activities that continue to the present time.

The advent of new information technology in Nigeria, as in many parts of the world, is creating an atmosphere where almost everybody is becoming a journalist of sorts. Apart from cell phones, which have taken telephonic communication away from being viewed as a luxury for the rich, other formats in the modern means of communication afford people the opportunity to make video footage of whatever is happening around them and forward the same to media outfits in what has been termed i-reporter. This is a form of dialogical communication that puts the media in the hands of all. In the same way, many media outfits now offer phone-in programs through which the audience is able to contribute to whatever issue is being discussed at any point in time.

The dialogical aspect of the new media depends on one's ability to acquire the necessary gadgets to perform this feat. In Nigeria where the unreliable supply of electricity has become entrenched in daily life, possession of inverters or a set of generators has been people's hope of staying up-to-date. The ability to have a functional Internet connection is also of paramount importance. Consequently, those without equal access to these gadgets, the "info-poor" as I explained earlier, depend on whatever is given to them by the so-called "info-rich". This digital divide does not allow for the kind of dialogue that is expected in a new digital age. The demographic that has been highly impacted by the digital age is youth.

Dialogue and Youth Identity in a Digital Age

The youth, citizens of the new media age, have embraced not only the novelty but also the challenges offered by the new media age. Basking in the privilege of their "netizenship" (that is, people born in the age of the Internet), and with the opportunities offered by the new media, which oftentimes remove the control hitherto given by parents and guardians, dialogue is seen in a different light in this digital age. One of the factors that affects dialogue in the present dispensation is the kind of identity young ones form through the way they employ the new media. The new media is not only readily available but also affordable to many, thereby exerting both positive and negative impacts on young minds. The kinds of personalities youths form today based on their media use affect human relationships on many fronts.

The issue of personality and identity formation has been a major concern among psychologists, sociologists, and those engaged in the study of human behavior. While acknowledging the fact that the concept of identity is multi-faceted, the renowned sociologist, Anthony Giddens, brings out two main types of identity, often discussed in his field of study as social identity and self-identity. For him, social identity is nothing but the characteristics that are attributed to an individual by others, while self-identity, which is the thrust of this section of the book, "refers to the process of self-development through which we formulate a unique sense of ourselves and our relationship to the world around us" (Giddens, 2005: 29). This present book explores these dimensions of identity with a view to understanding the influence of media use on youth online identity formation.

As I noted in previous chapters of this book, the way one views himself or herself affects internal dynamics of dialogue that occurs within the individual and the resultant external relationships with other persons. In this light, self-image and identity formation can be viewed as both sides of the same coin. One of the theories which explain online identity formation is the theory of Social Identity by Henri Tajfel and John Turner. They believe the human person is made up of several "selves" waiting to be explored and exhibited. These several selves come to the fore based on different social contexts, which trigger the individual to think, feel, and act on the basis of his personal, family, or national level of self.

In light of the aforesaid, one may talk of the level of education attained or social class as a condition for the type of self an individual exhibits. Building on an earlier work by Tajfel (1982), Tajfel and Turner hold that "our self-pride and self-esteem are products of the groups to which we belong since the groups give a sense of social identity" (2012). Social psychologists talk of in-group and out-group as ways of describing how we evaluate who we are and our relationship with others. In this context, we see a resonance with the JOHARI Window earlier examined in this book and how each of the quadrants affects how we see ourselves, one's model of communication, and the type of relationship produced by such model of communication.

Many studies in recent times point to a dichotomy that often exists between the kind of personality people display in the new social media and their real self in ordinary everyday life (Boyd & Ellison, 2007; Marwick & Boyd, 2011; Van Dijck, 2013; Kocak, 2013). A great number of persons want to portray the best image of themselves as seen in the type of display pictures on social network pages. There have been cases of marriages contracted online where the other party gets to know that the person he or she had been communicating with virtually is not in actual fact the kind of person in the display picture. Some refer to this as "packaging", a situation in which falsehood is celebrated online and to the detriment of reality.

The new media in general, and the social network sites in particular, have become in recent times, an "avenue for self-promotion, those who get acknowledgement from their peers are said to be influencers and as people manifest themselves online with regard to their skills and proficiency, they attract contracts, customers and employers" (Van Dijck, 2013: 203). Van Dijck had earlier postulated that social media profiles do not really reflect one's identity, rather they are "part and parcel of a power struggle between users, employers/employees and platform owners to steer online information and behavior" (2013: 112).

Koonin argues for the need to manage the reputation and identity of young adults in a social media environment by presenting the case of Leandra dos Santos, a white South African model, alleged to have posted a racist hate speech on her twitter profile after having a scuffle with a Black gentleman in a local market in 2012. This caused her not only to lose contracts, but it also generated other hate tweets from other persons (2013:76). This lady's reputation suffered a setback due to her wrong use of the social network. This shows that just as the online environment can be used for self-presentation and self-promotion, especially as in the case of Facebook and LinkedIn (Van Dijck, 2013:200), if not well managed, it could lead to self-destruction.

In light of the above, Koonin calls for: education, that is, media literacy; online ethics and legal awareness; seeing and managing the self as a brand; peer review; self-reflection practices; being given social grounding in morals and values and the importance of opinion leaders as ways of managing effective online identity (2013:89). Education in the use of media is very important since many people do not understand that anything posted online remains there even after you delete it. Everyone leaves a digital footprint online, which can be discovered even in years to come. These items posted online do not only reflect the kind of dialogue people have within themselves but also condition the kind of dialogue they stand to get from media consumers as in the case of dos Santos mentioned above.

The issue of intra-personal dialogue and online identity formation has also been linked to the idea of memory. The logic here is that a recall of who one is helps to fashion the kind of identity he or she exhibits. Konack argues that the history of memory can be divided into the following phases: pre-modern times, where relations between people and their past was natural; then the nineteenth, century when there was a fall of memory, only for relations between people and their past to be reconstructed through languages, monuments, archives, all geared towards the nation state (2013:206). He argues that while the state helps in the analysis of where we are coming from as a people and where we are going, the age of the nation state has been replaced with that of globalization, with its attendant characteristics (Konak, 2013: 206).

Mitszal commented on the effects of globalization on human identity when he argued: "...human society has moved from the oral to the written, print and now electronic cultures show that collective memory in the present age is shaped by technological changes in the means of communication" (2003:22). This movement in human civilization from the traditional to the modern and now the digital age has tremendous impacts on our thinking process, the model of communication we employ, and the effect of the two on the relationships we build.

The kind of identity that is formed by young persons today, and by extension the way they engage in dialogue, is so different from what occurred years ago. In the traditional societies, identity was "...fixed, solid, and stable. It was a function of social rules and a traditional system of myths as one is born, grows, and dies as a member of a particular clan where identity crisis was not an issue. Identity crisis is not an issue in this context since one grows up within the same cultural system in which he/she was socialized, and the elders are readily available to supply what might be missing in an individual's pool of knowledge. In modern times, identity has become mobile, personal, multiple and greatly dependent on innovations" (Konack, 2013: 211).

This was also the view of Kellner who earlier postulated that: "The modern self is aware of the constructed nature of identity and that one can always change and modify one's identity at will. One is also anxious concerning recognition and validation of one's identity by others. Further, modernity also involves a process of innovation, of constant turnover, and novelty" (1992: 142). Kellner therefore affirms that: "Modernity signifies the deconstruction of past forms of life, values, and identities, combined with the production of ever new ones" (1992:142).

In traditional societies, among most African cultures, for example, the child is socialized to always think about the kind of family he or she comes from before engaging in any act. In those kinds of societies, an individual is always told to remember "the child of whom you are." This has changed in the present social dispensation to the dictum of: "It's my life". Most times, young persons act as if they are accountable to no one, but should they run into any problems, they always find the way back to their families. As such, the modern person is constantly oscillating between different personalities of a being-in-community or an individual self.

Oftentimes, this oscillation is also assisted and aided by what the media offers at a particular instance. This has further shown human life to be a theatre of sorts. It is a kind of Hollywood experience where an actor plays one role today only to be given a completely opposite character the next time. In this vein, youth identity is often formed by the kind of media they employ. That is, identity of youths is at the mercy of the new media that functions as the director in this Hollywood-like experience with the capacity to alter roles assigned to young minds depending on the digital script being played out.

Thus, the youthful age is greatly associated with the period of life when the young mind desires to explore and experiment on many issues. Social scientists believe that a number of deviant behaviors are exhibited at this stage of life. In many instances, the young mind wants to do away with every form of authority and control by those he or she perceives as hindering his or her liberty and freedom so as to assert his or her own will. In this state of flux and novelty, young ones find a ready partner in the new media.

This is so, since, "the Internet has become a significant social laboratory for experimenting with the constructions and reconstructions of self that characterize postmodern life. In this virtual reality, we self-fashion and self-create. What kinds of personae do we make? What relation do these have to what we have traditionally thought of as the whole person? ... These questions can be addressed by looking at many different locations on the Internet" (Turkle, 1995: 180).

Therefore, the new media is creating a youth group that remains in perpetual flux as to the right kind of identity to form, the kind of relationships to have, and the model of communication to employ in dialogue. Just as we self-create online, do we not also self-destruct? With the inclusion of "like", "follow", "comment", etc., on many social network sites, those who use this media look for the kind of identity that will give them the best online followership. To this end, display pictures are changed following a comment made by a friend on the same page, and online posts are either left online or removed based on a favorable comment or otherwise. This identity formation links peoples of like-minds into a form of cyber-community or relationship.

Forming people into communities of like-minds has created a situation where dialogue is limited and myopic as groupthink is now the order of the day. Thus, Kwon & Wen hold that: "Social network sites build and verify social networks for the individuals and communities who share interests and activities with one another, or who are interested in exploring the interests and activities of others" (2010: 225). The caveat in this is that the kind of community so formed is devoid of broad and open perspectives. People belong to such virtual communities as long as they are told whatever they want to hear. Being told a contrary opinion, not minding if this is for the good of the person, causes many to exit the group. What form of identity is then being formed online? With this kind of identity, it is now very easy to disengage from any form of dialogue or "unfriend" anyone at the click of a button.

From the foregoing, it is obvious that social media has become an avenue for identity formation and the social network sites help people to fashion the kind of adult life they wish to lead by the kind of profile they create for themselves. Through the choice of pictures used, relationship status, favorite books, movies, religious view, and political angle, people now make their profile a digital body where people write about themselves (Zhao, Grasmuck & Martin, 2008; Boyd, 2008). This is so since: "In modern times, is not about who we are or where we come from, rather it has come to be about what we are going to be and how we are going to be represented" (Hall, 1996: 3).

The above view was buttressed by Mitszal, who argues that: "People use identity to make sense of themselves, of their activities, of what they share with others and how they differ from them" (2003: 132). Consequently, there is a close connection between the use of the new media, the kind of identity formed, and those we choose to engage in dialogue. This connection is further enhanced by the amount of time spent online. Continuous online presence has a lot of impact on the lives of youths who do various things online, ranging from the mundane to more serious online research for academic purposes.

The media are said to possess a gate-keeping power because they are able to shut out of public discourse certain issues, while at the same time some other issues are put on a platform where they are easily noticed and gain prominence. While other media like the television, radio, and newspaper do this to a large extent, the new media, exemplified in social network sites, have come to echo and take to Olympian heights whatever was hitherto done by the traditional platforms.

In the present dispensation, there is an information overload in this media-saturated society. Even when one does not desire to know about certain things, these pop up on their own once one is connected online. There are advertising companies whose products come up each time you are connected online, and once you click on such windows, you stand the chance of being lured into other sites you may not really desire.

Thus, consciously or unconsciously, the things that pop up online affect the way media users begin to see reality. Continuous online presence only cements the attitudinal change brought about by such media contents. Online communication therefore favors, to an extent, unreasoned dialogue, and communication with strangers is promoted through this medium. This has taken dialogue away from the traditional understanding of communication between persons in close proximity, whereby they possess some level of knowledge about one another. Due to the fact that people tend to dialogue with strangers who pop up online, many young persons have become preys to online perverts.

Again, unchecked online presence has lured many persons into becoming victims of cyber criminals. Unfortunately, many developing nations have been identified with online crime, which in Nigeria is known as, "Advanced Free Fraud". Living in Canada in the last couple of years, I have received phone calls from people claiming to be tax agents stating that I should make certain payments so as to avoid arrest. Some of the perpetrators of these crimes have been traced to some nations far away from Canada.

Moreover, there was a time when Nigeria was known with such taxonomies as "Yahooism", "Yahoozee", Yahoo-Yahoo", to mention but a few. All these point to cybercrime, which is otherwise known as 419 in Nigeria. The main issue here is that due to prolonged online presence, some individuals see the fast life of people in developed nations, and they desire to emulate such. They therefore devise means of hacking, cloning, and obtaining people's financial details online in a bid to swindle such unsuspecting individuals.

Not only do cyber criminals obtain people's information, some go outright to fake certain business transactions and ask their victims to pay into certain accounts before the deal can be sealed. In recent times, the practice has been to clone the website of some banks and write to customers of such banks that their online account has been compromised and, to block unauthorized transactions, the account owner should click a web link. Once the web link is clicked, all data in such an account is made available to the fraudsters. The gist here is that cybercrime, like many other crimes, survives in an atmosphere where there is little or no dialogue. When people share their experiences and ask advice of others, the propensity to fall victim is reduced.

In a study showcasing the type of behavior people learn online and the effects of this on their identity, Greece (2014) focused on a Greek Facebook group whose members post announcements on the group wall about impending learning events. Facebook, it is important to note, has become a "United Nations" of sorts due to the large number of users who cut across national, linguistic, and ethnic barriers. For the study by Greece, however, the groups were chosen because members look explicitly for learning activities and because the group does not constitute an online community of practice since the study's aim was to investigate the types of learning that occur through casual use of Facebook.

In this study, out of the 554 invitations sent to active members, only 250 (201 female and 49 male) responded to the study within the age bracket of 20-50 years. In his discussion of findings, Greece holds that half of the participants agreed that they (a) seek information about issues of interest by asking people on Facebook, (b) gain knowledge about issues of interest by asking other people on Facebook, (c) express their thoughts/ideas on their wall and get feedback that helps them to develop their thoughts/ideas further. Finally, more than seven out of ten participants agree that they use Facebook groups to keep updated about issues of interest (2014: 186).

Further, on the kind of identity formed through the use of social network sites, Greece confirms that: "Nearly one out of ten participants reported that they often present a different personality either in their profile or in chat discussions so as to promote themselves better, and about two out of ten claimed they learned how to get along with other people due to Facebook use" (2014: 193). This study confirms what I have been espousing above with regard to the behavioral change that can come with Internet use. An important feature of this change is in the aspect of dialogue.

Communication as we know it is all about sharing and relationship. Learning to get along with people through Facebook, as the study above confirms, can be seen both in positive and negative ways. In the first instance, Facebook and other social media have helped to connect people in various walks of life. There are occasions when former schoolmates, friends, or even family members rediscover one another through social media. On the contrary, the same media can lead to a form of anonymity, in which people hide behind the computer screen to communicate what they would not have done in person.

In another study that chronicles the status people maintain online and their attitudes and motivations, Shoenberger and Tandoc (2014) build on extant studies linking media use to gratification. It is pertinent to note as affirmed by Katz, Blumler & Gurevitch (1974), that the Uses and Gratification Approach has four basic categories of motivations derived from media use: diversion (drive to escape the doldrums of daily life); personal relationships (use media to forge companionship); personal identity (use media to understand and express oneself); and surveillance (use media to seek information about the environment). Thus, these categories of uses and gratification relate with social psychologists' theories that show that human persons have two motivational systems that operate independently of one another and inform the selection processes that assist with the survival of the species (Cacioppo, Gardner & Bernston, 1999).

The aforesaid can be further broadened to show how humans react to the survival instinct when the environment is favorable or otherwise. According to Shoenberger & Tandoc, "When the environment is conducive, the individual gathers food and procreates, and if not, the response is fight or flight" (2014: 221). The main point here is that attitudinal change is directly proportional to the amount of time spent online, and those who find gratification in what the new media has to offer maintain a constant presence therein, while those who do not find gratification take flight. Excessive presence online brings about a corresponding problem to the offline attitudes of the individual. This can lead to a situation where some find comfort in the online community, whereas day-to-day life, dialogue, and relationships suffer.

Nigeria ranks as one of the fastest developing nations in Africa. This development is seen not only in the social dimension but also in commerce and industry. In the field of communication and culture, Nollywood, the Nigerian version of American Hollywood and Indian Bollywood, has not only become a household name on the continent but also globally, with a capacity of showcasing the richness of Nigerian culture in movies and offering jobs to the teeming population in the nation. The cities of Lagos, Enugu, and Onitsha on a daily basis, witness an influx of young men and women nursing the dream of becoming stars in the Nigerian movie industry.

Again, the novelty of cellular phones in the wake of this millennium was a turning point for the nation. Hitherto, as earlier stated, ownership of telephone lines was a privilege reserved for the rich and influential. In the present dispensation, almost everyone has a handset, social status or educational level notwithstanding. Tella, Adetoro, and Adekunle noted that: "Before the year 2001, the number of connected phone lines in Nigeria was a mere 450,000 for an estimated population of 120 million people" (2009: 55). However, "...by 2008, various GSM service providers had approximately 59 million active subscribers in Nigeria and 'a teledensity' (a quantity of telephone lines in relation to residents) of 42%" (Taiwo, 2010: 2).

The present communications and information feat attained by the government of Nigeria was made possible through the launch of a Nigerian satellite, which catapulted communication in Nigeria to a digital precinct of Olympian heights. It is believed that: "With its launch on May 13, 2007, Nigerian NigComSat-1 was the first African geosynchronous communication satellite ... However, when this failed in orbit because it ran out of power on November 11, 2008, the need for another satellite became expedient. The second attempt was thus NigeriaSat-X and NigeriaSat-2 from Yasny, Russia" (Olusola, 2012: 232).

This historical excursion shows the steps Nigeria has taken to be media-compliant in this contemporary time. In fact, this major stride is echoed in the fact that the second aforementioned satellite was built by Nigerians! Availability of the new media in the hands of virtually everyone brought about an unprecedented media presence and its attendant consequences. One of the consequences of this media presence has been the over-reliance on whatever the digital means has to offer to the detriment of social relations among people. In this situation, authentic dialogue and face-to-face communication are major victims.

The fact that authentic dialogue suffers in the present digital media-scape can be further seen in the unchecked self-expression and assertions new media offer. Online dialogue suffers today through people who are not able to accept divergent opinions but turn the online platform into avenues for insulting others and promoting hate. In this light, Rose-Redwood et al. hold that: "Dialogue can also be weaponized and used as a tactic of harassment, intimidation, and symbolic violence, particularly through the use of social media" (2018: 112).

A practical example is a certain platform on Facebook known as "24/7 Nigeria News Update", which is presently used by many Nigerians. This is meant to be a platform where news of happenings within and outside the nation is brought to Nigerians through their phones or any other means with which they access their Facebook account. In many instances, this means has been turned into a place to insult persons who hold contrary opinions. Quite a number of offensive comments are written on this website. This becomes disheartening, considering the fact that an average Nigerian is brought up with the idea of respect for elders and that, even if one does not agree with the opinion of such elders, there are subtle ways of making one's contrary opinion known.

The present dispensation, where caution is thrown to the wind in this web-dialogue as some actually engage in a war of words, which could have actually transformed into a real clash should there be any physical proximity between those communicating, is not limited to Nigeria or Africa alone. The wrong use of the digital media as a way to castigate other persons on account of their contrary opinion has found a home in many parts of the world. Like never before, this is creating enmity between persons and providing annoyance for people in the cyber community.

Rose-Redwood et al. commented on the same situation in the United States, where the current political dispensation has polarized the country to a large extent. In their view, the present polarization has led to a situation where, "...a single tweet online can generate an avalanche of hateful counter-speech, ad hominem attacks, doxing, other forms of personal harassment by Internet trolls, and a litany of 'alternative facts', and spurious or ill-(in) formed argument" (2018: 177). In essence, hiding behind the screen of the virtual world, many persons insult, malign, and castigate others. There have been reports of cyber-bullying resulting in untold harm to people's dignity and even leading to death in some instances. This, surely, is not the kind of dialogue that builds communities; rather it destroys individuals and communities.

In sum, this chapter has been saddled with the task of espousing the kind of dialogue that has been engendered through the present digital age and the means of communication at our disposal. We have seen that communication is the right of everyone and, most importantly, that the digital age has brought tremendous change to the way people communicate and dialogue. With practical examples from different parts of the globe, we have seen that, just as the new media can be used for positive ends, they also have negative effects. It was argued here that unchecked and prolonged online presence can reshape the attitudes of people and their ability to engage in traditional face-to-face dialogue.

Citing the works of scholars from various fields of human endeavor, this chapter has shown that, to a large extent, modern social network sites condition how people, especially the youth, see themselves and the manner with which they relate with those around them. It was said that it is not enough to have a democratized and dialogical means of digital communication, but that these modern means have some lessons to be learned from traditional media. In this sense, communication in the digital age will not be just a means of passing information, but most importantly, will be an avenue to dialogue, get involved in the lives of people, and jointly build enduring communities. How can this done? What do we need to rediscover the importance of authentic dialogue in our present digital society? This will be the thrust of the next chapter of this book.

CHAPTER SIX

———————•———————

Rediscovering the Import of Dialogue

In tandem with all that has been said above, it is obvious that there is need in present human society to rediscover the importance of effective dialogue in human relationships. The thesis of this book has been that a great deal of everyday communication stems from our inner dialogue, intra-personal discourse, or thought processes, which go a long way to shape and direct other forms of communication and the relationships we have with people. Just as we saw in the third chapter of this book, there is more to listening than we usually envision; similarly, dialogue needs to be given a more serious consideration in our daily encounters.

It is not enough for us to dialogue; we need to ensure that the kind of dialogue we engage in is effective in building not just the individuals communicating, through feedback, but also that dialogue enhances life in the community as a whole. This is the type of dialogue which: "…requires the right people to talk about the right issues in the right way and at the right time and place" (Nixon: 2012: 57).

In chapter two of this book which enumerated issues around development communication, I showed that efforts at helping local communities often fail, because those who should be involved in the very first phase of any development project, that is, identification of problems and then charting the way to resolving them are oftentimes excluded from the dialogue table. This happens when external agents, to the exclusion of locals, dominate change and development initiatives that affect local communities. The adverse effects of this can only be imagined. Sometimes, it leads to the situation of putting the cart before the horse with regard to prioritizing the needs of the people, if not, in dire cases, a total exclusion of the real needs of the people from the equation.

In essence, rediscovering the importance of dialogue in communication is an effort at taking dialogue back to its root as a form of bridge building and meaning-making, with the involvement of everyone in the communication process. This begins with the intra-personal level through which people are able to process their thoughts, voice such thoughts in dialogical communication with others, and in a participatory way, jointly find solutions to what began as a fruit of that intra-personal dialogue. This is important since the participatory and dialogical understanding of communication is in contrast to the former idea of communication as the hypodermic needle aimed at injecting ideas into people without their own contribution. This earlier notion still rears its ugly head in our society today, and digital media has much more to do in combating this.

The digital society has brought a great deal of development to humanity, as I mentioned in the previous chapter, and has given rise to immediacy in communication. There has been, at the same time, an astronomical increase in consumerism and advertising, which serve the main purpose of influencing people's behavior. The rise in the way the media is used for propaganda and political ideologies is gradually, albeit at a very fast speed, taking humanity back to the 1930s and 1940s, when communication was used to spread the news that those in power wanted the rest of the population to believe. The digital divide between the info-rich and info-poor is widening the chasm between these two groups with regard to availability of information. Since information is said to be power, the one who possesses it always has the upper hand against others who may not have the same access to information and are thereby said to be powerless with regard to information.

The above view is in tandem with Harold Lasswell who, shortly after the Second World War, published his view on communication as: "Who says what, to whom, through which medium and with what effect" (1948:37). This can be simply explained starting with, "Who says what." This is the person who initiates the communication process and according to this view, this person is very important as well as whatever he or she says.

The second aspect of this view, "to whom", refers to the receptor of the communication. The receiver is seen in the transmission model to be a passive object, without any capacity to make meaning or respond to the given communication. The receptor here is reduced to having no rational capacity to give feedback, but can only absorb whatever is injected by the initiator of the communication. The third aspect of this understanding of communication deals with the channel of passing information on. In the 1940s, the radio was at its peak as a mass medium in many parts of the world. The radio, at that time, was seen as an improvement on the telephonic means of communication that held sway and also on newspapers, which were humanity's first attempt at mass communication.

Consequently, those who controlled the radio medium did not only have the gate-keeping power of what gets into media content, they also influenced what program would be broadcast to what audience and at what time. This aligns with the dictum that has been credited to the Canadian communications expert, Marshall McLuhan, who, in his 1964 article about understanding the media, stated that: "The medium is the message." This highlights the fact that the medium does not only shape, but also determines, how a media message is received. The radio did all of this in the time of Lasswell.

The highpoint of Lasswell's definition of communication is in the last part: "with what effect". Here, the main agenda of the transmission notion of communication is to bring about response in the receiver of media messages. Communication is not seen here as meaning-making; rather, its purpose is to influence, change, and affect another person. In this view, therefore, dialogue is hampered and the human persons who should share ideas so as to better their communities become the victims.

In the preceding chapters of this book, I have shown the various instances in which this linear transmission and hypodermic view of communication is still prevalent today in families, in offices, among friends, and even in religious circles. This happens when one person tends to dominate every discussion and wants everyone else to accept his or her point of view at all cost. We may have witnessed occasions where certain persons want to be the center of attention at every event. They want to take the position of the bride at every wedding; the celebrant at every birthday; and even the corpse at every funeral.

Such persons think they have the best idea in every circumstance and others must shut up and listen, drink from their "reservoir of knowledge", and learn from their "staple of wisdom". In this case, dialogue becomes just a way to fulfill all righteousness since the endpoint of every discussion has been predetermined, predestined, and preplanned. Their intention is one and only – inject whatever ideas they have into others who are considered less able to either critically process the information given or give the needed feedback. This hypodermic transmission model of communication is diametrically opposed to the effective dialogue this book highlights.

In view of what communication has become in recent times, with people using even online media as avenues to promote their own ideas and being ready to hurl insults at any other person who has a contrary opinion, Pope Francis gave his message for the 54th World Communications Day, which was celebrated on May 24, 2020 on the theme, "That You May Tell Your Children and Grandchildren: Life Becomes History". World Communications Day has been celebrated since after the second Vatican Council's document on Social Communication – *Inter Mirifica*.

All the popes have issued documents on this day ever since its first celebration, and each of their letters speaks to the particular situation confronting humanity at a given time. In tandem with all that has been happening around the world lately and how the media have been employed to fuel hatred, falsehood, and division among peoples, Pope Francis reminds humanity of our inter-connectedness and the need for stories that build up instead of tearing down.

Pope Francis began this letter by saying: "Amid the cacophony of voices and messages that surround us, we need a human story that can speak of ourselves and of the beauty all around us. A narrative that can regard our world and its happenings with a tender gaze. A narrative that can tell us that we are part of a living and interconnected tapestry. A narrative that can reveal the interweaving of the threads which connect us to one another." The main text of this letter is taken from the book of Exodus (10:2), where the

Israelites were reminded to tell their offspring all that God did for them.

Building on that text of scripture, the pope holds that God is, at the same time, a creator and narrator. God was the first to create and tell the human story. God's story is ever renewed, and it renews humanity. The compendium of this story is to be found in the first printed matter, the Bible. The Holy Book contains many stories, but all these stories culminate in Jesus Christ. The story of Jesus is not written on tablet stones but on human hearts (2 Cor. 3:3).

The pope affirms that it is when we allow our own stories to be aligned with Christ's that our own story becomes a part of that great story. He says, "With the gaze of the great storyteller – the only one who has the ultimate point of view – we can then approach the other characters, our brothers and sisters who are with us as actors in today's story." This explains why I devoted a great part of this book to storytelling. In this book, I have shared stories I learnt in childhood through cultural gatherings as a kid and through TV dramas.

Moreover, I also narrated my experiences growing up in high school and the book features concrete stories of persons I have encountered in my ministry to God's people across various continents in the last 20 years. In these stories, the main point I have underscored is what the pope affirms in his letter – that humanity is more connected than we can ever imagine. All it takes is for us to listen to our inner voice – that dialogue that happens within, in order to more effectively listen to the joys and hopes, the fears and anxieties of our brothers and sisters; and thereby build a better human relationship.

Skills Needed towards Authentic Dialogue

Nixon proposes five skills that anyone who wishes to engage in efficient and authentic dialogue needs to possess. These are what he called PRESA – Presence, Respect, Expression, Suspending, and Absorbing (2012: 73-74). Being present has turned out to be lacking in many communication experiences today. This is because people get distracted through many factors. Can you remember the many times a very serious conversation has been disrupted by cell phones ringing or notification from one social platform or another on the same device?

I have witnessed occasions when people got out of a church to go and receive a phone call. If this kind of distraction by an external source (that is, a phone call) can happen within the sacred space of a Church, imagine the great many disturbances that are internal – that is, our thoughts. Oftentimes, these thoughts distract people from being present in a communication process. In essence, even though people are physically present, they can also at the same time be mentally absent. To be effective, therefore, communicating parties must be fully present so as to receive both verbal and non-verbal communication cues and thus be able to give appropriate feedback.

The second aspect of Nixon's postulation, "Respect", can be viewed from the point of the common dictum: "Respect is Reciprocal." Even the Bible holds that people should do unto others what they want to be done to them (Mt. 7: 12). Many world religions believe in this Golden Rule of treating others the way one would want to be treated. The same is what Nixon talks about in this second aspect of his postulation. This is concerned with the need to understand that everyone comes to the dialogue with an idea to share with others, and authentic dialogue happens when no one's idea is considered superior to those of others. This is contrary to the hypodermic notion of communication that I had earlier talked about. Without respect for one another, real conversation and dialogue cannot take place.

The third aspect of Nixon's idea is "Expression". Since communication is not only about verbal expression of ideas, it is important to note that people may choose to express themselves in various ways, including sign language, emotional communication, body language, etc. As I pointed out in the earlier chapters of this book, a media message, for example, a pictorial message, can be polysemic; that is, having both surface and depth meaning. One needs to oscillate between the first and second level of signification in order to know what a media message expresses. This movement across the various layers of expression should not be done in a hurry so as to avoid hasty and wrong conclusions. The ability to understand these various aspects of communication can be the seed of effective dialogue.

In the fourth category, Nixon presents "Suspending" as that which occurs when we do away with hitherto held beliefs and ideas when a superior argument is presented. He believes that, for dialogue to be effective, we must be ready to let go of our ideas when presented with a better argument. Unfortunately, many hold tenaciously to whatever they once believed, to the extent that their self-growth and development are hindered. Although change often takes time to be fully effected, it is important to be open to receiving positive changes in dialogue.

Some persons easily accept change, while others take some time to weigh the options before giving in to change. For others, things must always be as they have always been. Our ability to suspend former ideas when a better one is presented makes for good dialogue. We must note that the person who suspends his/her idea today may be the one with the best idea tomorrow. As such, no one can lay claim to having the best idea all the time, and everyone should be ready to let go of previously held ideas.

The final category by Nixon is "Absorb", which occurs in dialogue when people internalize what has been shared, make it their own, and give appropriate feedback. As such, absorbing is not just taking in everything hook, line, and sinker, but rationally processing what has been shared and giving a reasoned response in the form of feedback. In my years of teaching at the post-graduate level, I found out that some students arrived with the idea of regurgitating whatever the lecturer gave them in class.

While some students easily absorb and answer questions in their own words, others practice what we jokingly called "Xerox". This is so, since their scripts look like a photocopy of the teacher's notes. For dialogue to be effective, our ability to internalize a shared idea and give reasoned feedback cannot be overemphasized. These five steps, according to Nixon, do not occur in a static manner, but they are constantly evolving since dialogue itself is a process.

Dialogue: An On-going Process

As I mentioned above, dialogue is not a once-for-all act but a continuous process. A break in the chain of this process affects the communicating parties and may unleash untold hardship on nations. We see this in the experience of South Africa, a nation that, after many years of apartheid and the imprisonment of Nelson Mandela for 27 years, decided to move forward by healing the wounds of the past.

To do this, South Africans constituted the Truth and Reconciliation Commission under the Chairmanship of Archbishop Desmond Tutu, in 1996. This Commission was a way of engaging the kind of dialogue that would ensure that the pains and hardships of the past would never be repeated. Working under three committees of Human Rights Violations, Reparation and Rehabilitation, and an Amnesty Committee, this Commission discovered that more than 20,000 persons had been victims of human rights violations.

Employing the Restorative justice system, the Commission tried to heal the wounds of the past, while at the same time channelling a new path for the nascent democracy in South Africa. When Mandela, under whose presidency of that nascent democracy the Truth and Reconciliation Commission was inaugurated, left power after a single term in office, the departure of the Madiba, as he was fondly called, led the way for Thabo Mbeki, who then became President. This period saw a new South Africa with developments in many aspects and a new level of recognition on the world stage.

After Mbeki, came the short presidency of Kglema Motlanthe, before Jacob Zuma, who later faced a lot of challenges and was accused of many negative things by his compatriots, came on board. The effort at nation building in the nascent South African democracy that was achieved in the years of Mandela and Mbeki witnessed a major setback recently in the ongoing presidency of Cyril Ramaphosa.

Towards the last quarter of 2019, South Africa found itself in the global news, albeit not for something positive, but rather, for xenophobic attacks on fellow Africans. These attacks led to the death of many immigrants of African descent while businesses of many more were attacked, looted, and destroyed. The carnage was so severe that a privately owned commercial airline company in Nigeria volunteered a fleet of flights to airlift Nigerians who wanted to escape the threat of death at the hands of their fellow Africans. This wave of hatred and destruction was propelled by a breakdown in dialogue due to the belief that immigrants were taking jobs meant for South Africans and were responsible for the failing economy and high crime rate in the nation.

It is disheartening to note that these erroneous claims were not only propagated by average people on the streets, but most importantly, by some politicians and traditional chiefs. It was reported that these elites did much in constantly reducing the number of foreign nationals allowed to legally enter South Africa. In their view, a reduction in immigration would solve their national problems. To say the least, this is un-African, and there has been no scientific data to back this erroneous claim.

The recent wave of xenophobic attacks brought worldwide condemnation, and many leaders of nations boycotted the World Economic Forum on Africa, a summit that was held in Cape Town about this time. What the experience of South Africa shows is the deterioration in dialogue and the efforts at building a new South Africa that had been charted in the mid-1990s.

I remember as a young high-school student in the 1980s in Nigeria that, written at the front of every classroom, was the caption: "Apartheid is a Crime against Humanity". This was borne out of the South African experience and many nations on the continent rose up to support South Africa financially and otherwise during the apartheid era. In a series of meetings in the 1980s and 1990s, African nations and other nations around the globe dialogued to find the best way to set South Africa free from the shackles of the colonial powers.

It is disheartening to see how the same South Africa has turned a deaf ear to dialogue, but has taken up arms against other Africans. Nevertheless, this calls for a better understanding of dialogue as a continuous process. It is time to rediscover the seed of dialogue that was planted in South Africa in the mid-1990s as a way of taking that nation to Olympian heights and its rightful place among the committee of nations, not only in Africa but the world at large. The magic is in continuous and constant dialogue.

Just like in the case of South Africa, where a minority with access to money and power held the majority of the population ransom for many years, we see a repeat of the same situation in present day society where the tyranny of the one with the loudest voice is one of the major banes of present civilization. We now live in a society where people wish to espouse their own ideas without the readiness to listen to that of another person. The words "hater", "homophobic", "judging" are thrown around today at the slightest opportunity. While not denying the fact that the aforementioned are realities in any human society, the rate at which everything is thrown under the umbrella of such terms is alarming and scary.

The situation is worsened by the various ideological stances that have found breeding grounds in our citadels of learning. The universities have become places where politicians, lobby groups, and interest groups brainwash young minds into groupthink and rejection of opposing views. There have been occasions when graduating classes turn their backs on someone invited to deliver the valedictory lecture just because they disagree with his or her political or religious view. Intolerance and refusal to dialogue with opposing views have found a home in our present society at a rate one never imagined before. This is so unfortunate, since the university is supposed to be a place for cross-pollination of ideas. As it is said, "From the Gown to the Town"; whatever happens in the ivory towers is supposed to be reflected in the society at large.

Many parents can attest to the changes they see in their children when they return from the universities. To the glory of God, a great many of these changes are positive. On the other hand, some parents have had occasion to ask if this was the same child they sent to the university a couple of months or years before. I have had occasion to discuss with parents who express disbelief and pain at what has become of their children when they return from the universities. While some parents try to navigate the situation by avoiding certain discussions with these young and fertile minds, other parents confront the elephant in the room. The result of this confrontation, most times, is not pleasing. One thing I always say to parents in such situations is to take cognizance of the context within which dialogue takes place. The Yorubas of Nigeria have a saying that can be translated to mean, "There are occasions when we have things to say but no time to fully express ourselves and at other occasions, we have all the time in the world but there is nothing to say." In this dictum, the idea is to understand when to engage in salient dialogue with people. The context, content, time, and place of dialogue is very important. If people take note of this in family dialogue, a great many problems arising from people's inability to listen to one another will be addressed, if not completely solved.

As we try to rediscover the import of dialogue in family life, we need to generally ask, "What is the ultimate purpose of dialogue? It is often said that every human act should be backed by reason. One of the sayings I heard from one of my university lecturers many years ago is that: "No one is ideologically neutral." I have alluded to this earlier in this book when I affirmed that we all come to the process of dialogue with myriad past experiences, present realities, and future expectations. As such, certain unavoidable questions which can guide our involvement in any dialogue process include: Why I am engaged in this dialogue, at this time, on this topic, with this person, and to what end? Having these questions, especially questions concerning the end point of every dialogue, brings to the fore the importance of this process.

To this end, Rose-Redwood et al. query: "Is the goal to ultimately reach consensus through rational deliberation, or is it to acknowledge that dissensus is inherent to scholarship and political endeavors, with dialogue then serving as a means of critically and constructively engaging with difference and disagreement?" (2018: 112) While consensus is in itself not intrinsically negative, it is important to note that, if far stretched, it can lead to groupthink; that is, a situation in which everyone tends to see things from the same angle and a dissenting opinion is considered to be someone attempting to rock the boat. On the contrary, the second dimension of Rose-Redwood et al's argument claims that dialogue will be most authentic when it acknowledges difference and engages this constructively.

Dialogue and Conflict Management

Suffice to ask, especially in situations when dialogue appears to be uncomfortable and may lead to misunderstanding: How can dialogue of differences be constructively engaged? As I highlighted above, there are occasions when unavoidable dialogues have rocked the boat in many families, among friends, and with colleagues in offices. With the COVID-19 pandemic, which rocked the entire world in the wake of 2020 and the stay-at-home orders from government officials, there were reports of tensions, misunderstandings, and even domestic violence as couples stayed together within the confines of their homes more than they usually did. To this end, Rose-Redwood et al. argue that: "Spaces of dialogical encounter are potential sites of conviviality and mutual aid, yet they can also be arenas of conflict, struggle, and antagonism" (2018:115).

The question then is: What do we do when dialogue goes sour, and how do we handle conflicts that may arise from such a situation? Do we just avoid such dialogue altogether and pretend that all is well or do we confront the "elephant in the room", get to the bottom of the issue, and even if the boat is rocked, we come out better? The fear of backlash has hampered some employees in voicing their intra-personal dialogue, which could have resulted in increased productivity in the workplace. Sometimes, what they wish to say may be for the good of the company but, feeling unsure of how their opinion may be received and in fear of losing their jobs, they may remain silent when they should share their ideas with others. Suffice to say, conflict pervades every aspect of human life, but the way it is handled shows how effective or otherwise dialogue has been.

Conflict often arises when there is a struggle over opposing ideas, values, or limited resources. We see this in families, offices, and many other aspects of life when there is one action that is incompatible with another – when one action is seen as preventing, obstructing or interfering with another in such a way that it makes that other less effective. A great many conflicts on the societal level arise from a struggle over status and power. We keep seeing this in the political dispensations across the world where opposing parties see nothing good in any action of the ruling party. No nation can make real progress if there is not an opposition party to engage in oversight duties and rein in the powers of the ruling party. If the opposition party constantly and perpetually sees nothing good in the party in power, however, this does not make for the healthy competition needed to build up nations.

With regard to dialogue, most conflicts begin on the ideational level. That is, when people are involved in dialogue towards making a decision that requires presentation and testing of various ideas, the differences arising from the many ideas, if not well handled, can result in conflict. Although many view conflict as something detrimental to the communication process, it can be useful if well handled. For example, conflict helps to increase involvement in a communication process; the more important an issue is to us, the more we tend to dialogue about it. Imagine how animated you become when talking about a particular sports team you support. Again, without conflict, one may not know what others feel about an idea or any given situation. As such, conflicts present fertile outlets for hostility that reveal deep-seated animosity, and in a supportive environment, this knowledge can be channeled towards growth.

Although conflicts arise for various reasons, they differ in intensity. With regards to conflicts arising from an ideational perspective, the intensity of the conflict is often dependent on the relative attractiveness of the options available for consideration. That is, in a situation where people are in dialogue concerning two opposing ideas, there is need to examine the level of importance of each of the ideas. In a situation whereby they are of equal importance, then it becomes harder to make a choice, and the conflict arising from this will be of higher intensity than in the case of opposing ideas where one is of more importance than the other. Whatever may be the source or the level of intensity of a conflict, the fact remains that, like every other thing in life, conflict could have both functional and dysfunctional effects on the people engaged in dialogue.

A conflict is said to be functional when the situation is skillfully managed as people work through differences. On the contrary, a dysfunctional conflict arises when communicating parties hold tenaciously to their previously held ideas and see opposing views as enemies to be conquered rather than another side of the same coin. To functionally manage conflict, among the many methods scholars have proposed, I am underlining five approaches for consideration here. These are: forcing, withdrawal, smoothing, compromise, and confrontation problem solving. People differ with regard to prioritizing these methods, and I believe one method may suit a particular situation more than the other. In this light, I will explain each of the methods, starting with forcing.

Forcing has to do with the practice of making your point of view in such a strong way that you convince the other person with whom you are in dialogue to accept your position. The idea of forcing here is not to engage in any physical or cohesive method; rather, it entails making a strong argument that sweeps the other arguments under the carpet. This was the kind of dialogue employed by great minds in the Greco-Roman world as I mentioned in the first chapter of this book.

The second, withdrawal, has to do with retreating from the argument. This can happen if there is a superior idea presented to negate your previously held idea. To step back should not be taken as a sign of inferiority; rather, it takes a strong person to recognize a better argument and accept it. The fact that one steps back in an instance does not mean the other person whose idea was accepted today may not be the one to step back tomorrow. The focus here is on superior argument, the person who makes it notwithstanding.

The third way of managing conflict is smoothing. As the name implies, this involves downplaying the conflict source. This could be the difference in ideas between persons in dialogue, while emphasizing the positive common interest or downplaying the importance of a scarce commodity that could become the source of conflict. When people downplay the difference in ideas or any other issue that may cause conflict, it emphasizes the fact that, no matter how different people think they are, there is some common ground, which if explored can bring about an effective dialogue process. I am one of those who believe that the main problem with the world today is not about our differences but our indifference. We have become so indifferent to one another that we often fail to see common ground to be explored. Smoothing calls for an emphasis on common interest as a way of managing conflict.

Compromise is the fourth method, in which each person in a dialogue gives something and gets a little back. In this situation, people must be ready to let go of some of their previously held ideas, while at the same time accept something from the other person. This is a form of equilibrium, which I earlier talked about with regard to Systems Theory in the second chapter of this book. This equilibrium sustains and maintains the process of dialogue.

The final stage of conflict management here is confrontation problem solving, which is when persons in dialogue are encouraged to direct their energies towards solving a problem and not to attack the other person or persons through confrontation. This is what I elucidated in the chapter that talks about digital media use and how people hide behind computer screens to attack anyone who expresses a contrary opinion to theirs. This also happens not only in the virtual but also in the real world of families, offices, and other avenues of human relationship.

In these stages, we see that if conflict is well managed, it can bring about a better process of dialogue. The important thing to note here is that just as there are efficient ways to manage conflict, there are dysfunctional ways of managing conflict. Some scholars believe that unhealthy ways of approaching conflict include blaming the other person, tending to be too general when addressing issues instead of clearly stating one's point of view, and avoiding conflict outright. This last example is what many persons tend to practice, not knowing that they are simply postponing the day of doom.

In order to avoid conflict, some persons practice what I call "graveyard peace". This is a situation in which the dead maintain their individual vaults without having anything to do with the person buried in the next grave. This is no peace at all. It is always better to dialogue even when the issue at hand brings about some discomfort, leading to conflict. The important thing is to know how best to manage the conflict in such a way that those in dialogue will better understand the issue at hand or themselves.

Improving Dialogue Effectiveness

Despite the reality of conflict in everyday conversation and dialogue, communication in general, and dialogue in particular, is an ongoing process and, no matter the level one may think one has attained presently, there is a need to improve this very important aspect of human relationship. Even in intra-personal dialogue, which forms the basis of other types of communication, conflict is rampant. The fact that conflicts occur in our intra-personal, inter-personal, and other forms of communication calls for us to find ways we can become more effective in the process of dialogue and not allow conflict to ruin this vital aspect of life. From the communication point of view, the following are ways scholars agree we can improve how we dialogue with one another:

Positiveness: Oftentimes, as mentioned earlier, people enter the process of dialogue with a particular bias or prejudice, leading to their being judgmental of other persons or situations. In being judged, many persons shut themselves off and avoid dialogue altogether. To avoid this, it is helpful to be positive in dialogue. Positiveness is otherwise called complimenting. That is, you give a positive attitude toward both the communication act you are doing and that of the other person. This act of complimenting the other is not the same as flattery. Giving compliments is not for you to say what is not true in order to boost the ego of the other; rather, it is a way of making the other person understand that you value whatever he or she has to say.

An example of complimenting someone with whom you are engaged in dialogue is when you cite a similar experience you may have had that corresponds with what the other person is saying. Again, compliments may be seen in the sense that you acknowledge the prowess of the speaker over an action, which, in truth, you may not have been able to perform. This simple act encourages the speaker to further engage in the dialogue. For example, my very first and last time on a roller coaster was a couple of years ago due to how scared I felt on it. Each time I hear some of my friends planning to go on a roller coaster and narrating the "excitement" of the same, brings compliments from me to them. Although this example may seem trivial, many dialogues start from the mundane and proceed to big life-changing situations. It is therefore important to be positive in every aspect of dialogue.

Openness: A lot was said about openness in the JOHARI Window, examined in the fourth chapter. I explained then how there is a need to move from the hidden, blind, and unknown quadrant to the open self. Building on this and the chapter that examined listening, openness involves a readiness to listen to the other person and empathize with him/her. You may not agree with the feelings of the person with whom you are in dialogue, but there is a need to at least admit that he/she has a right to feel the way he/she does. The need to be open to the feelings and emotions of others has many implications for an effective dialogue process. As this book affirms, communication is a process and what goes around, comes around. The empathy one shows to others today may come in handy should one be in need of the same subsequently.

As earlier said, the meaning-making act of communication and dialogue oscillates between the originator of the message and the receptor, who gets the message, makes meaning out of it, and sends feedback to the originator. The way each one is viewed in this cyclical process will affect how well the process unfolds. If the originator is not open to the feelings of the receptor, he or she stands the chance of the receptor being blind to the feelings of the originator when giving feedback. Just as there is a need to be open to feelings, there is also the need to be open to change that occurs in relationships. As communication shifts between originator and receptor, a lot of changes occur, and the ability to listen to these verbal and non-verbal clues will greatly enhance the dialogue process. In the same way, failure to listen to these clues will be detrimental to the communication process.

Supportiveness: As the name implies, this is the act of being there for the other. Everything about communication and dialogue is about bridge building and recognizing that no one is an island unto him/herself, since we all need one another. As espoused in earlier chapters of this book, bridge-building is one of the main tenets of the Christian faith, and most of the main religions of the world teach love and fellow-feeling. The need to be supportive of one another is also expressed in stories, songs, and other cultural avenues of human socialization. One such song that I grew up enjoying singing is the evergreen music by the American singer-songwriter, Bill Withers: "Lean on Me". The lyrics of this song affirm that there are times when we all have pain and, as such, we lean on one another since soon enough the one who helps now may be the one in need of assistance later.

Applied to the process of dialogue, this means that those engaged in the process should be there for each other by avoiding evaluative dispositions while embracing descriptive attitudes. We cannot overstate the fact that, when engaged in the process of dialogue, we need to focus on the problem rather than the person of the other party; that is, a situation when people ignore the main issues at hand to engage in what is known as *"argumentum ad hominem"*. On the contrary, to be supportive is to encourage the other to be the best he/she can be. The positive effect of this on dialogue cannot be over-emphasized. The shoulder that leans on you for strength today may be the same to hold you up should you be in need tomorrow.

Equality: The fact that we live in a world that is divided along many lines is no secret. The reality of the many dividing lines has become more obvious in recent times with the current political situation in many parts of the world. Social media and, unfortunately, some cable news network providers promote things that divide us rather than those that unite us. The division that is created in humanity has brought about a situation in which some persons feel they are better than others.

The term "equality" is not employed here to play down our differences in terms of gender, social status, and other intrinsic factors, but the fact remains that there is a connecting cord for humanity; that cord reminds us that we all belong to one race, the human race. The Christian faith holds that, despite our differences in appearance, we are all made in the image and likeness of God and endowed with the same dignity. The United Nations' Universal Declaration of Human Rights affirms that the equal dignity of all persons should be proclaimed from rooftops in the present dispensation.

One point I have emphasized in this book is that communication is a process that occurs between the originator and receptor of a communication message, with feedback, which then initiates another cycle of the process. This entails the sharing of ideas and decision-making in relationships. When people in dialogue see themselves as equal in dignity as humans, they jointly work to sustain the communication process.

Dialogue suffers when one person considers another person to be inferior and must just accept hook, line, and sinker whatever the originator has to say. We can all relate to this in past experiences in which one person tends to dominate discussion in the office, family gatherings, or among our group of friends. How did you feel at such a time? Some individuals go to the extent of making every other person look silly, claiming, albeit erroneously, that they alone have the correct idea in every given situation.

Value: An important tool in affirming the equal dignity of persons in dialogue is to acknowledge the value of each other. Generally, most relationships are entered into because you see value in the other person, but over the years, this may begin to dwindle or is taken for granted. As it is said, "familiarity breeds contempt". Moreover, we live at a time when some people, unfortunately, place more value on material things over and above the human person. We see this at play even during pandemics.

In the COVID-19 pandemic, there are alleged stories of relief materials in terms of money or food stuffs donated by governments all over the world to citizens in poorer countries and how some of those monies ended up in the private coffers of those responsible for the common good. They do this while the majority of people wallow in abject poverty on account of lockdown to curtail the spread of the virus. In some African nations at this time, the sight of people struggling to pick loaves of bread from moving buses to feed their family was, to say the least, unimaginable and demeaning.

In the aftermath of the #ENDSARS protest in October 2020 in Nigeria and the looting and destruction of private and public properties by hoodlums who infiltrated the peaceful protest as a way of disrupting their just agitation, these hoodlums have been linked to certain politicians. The ugly situation culminated in the shooting and killing of peaceful protesters at Lekki Toll Plaza in Lagos, Nigeria by persons suspected to be members of the military who first denied their presence at the venue only to agree they were there but fired blank shots at protesters.

In the ensuing imbroglio, we also witnessed with dismay how the masses discovered relief materials and food items meant to be shared with citizens on account of COVID-19 that were hoarded away in warehouses across Nigeria. In view of this inhumanity to fellow humans, there is need, therefore, to renew the value and dignity of the human person in order to rediscover our common humanity and to sustain any dialogue process.

As I have shown in earlier chapters of this book, the process of communication is influenced by our upbringing, socialization, education, past experiences, etc. With this arsenal of tools at our disposal, no communication or dialogue process is without value. If such then is the case, persons who are engaging in dialogue need to appreciate this value. Even if the other person says something you do not agree with, it does not reduce the value of the speaker. I mentioned earlier the need to separate the idea from the person who espouses the idea.

On the contrary, there are many instances when people "throw out the baby with the bath water". This is a saying that depicts a situation in which people go the extra mile of rejecting in total, not just an idea, but also the person who presents it. For dialogue to be effective, therefore, persons engaged in the process have to recognize and appreciate the value of one another.

Involvement: Originally, communication began with people in close proximity sharing ideas. This has since been replaced with the present digital media where the new means of communication have erased the spatio-temporal hindrances in communication, since people can now share ideas across the globe at the click of a computer mouse. Our society has moved from being a global village to becoming a global living room. This, as argued earlier, has brought immediacy and unprecedented feedback to the communication process.

In this same age, involvement in the same process continues to dwindle. The citizens of this digital age have been called many names, including "netizens", since they were born in the age of the

Internet. Some others refer to them as "People of the Thumb", since many young persons engage their thumbs in texting and generally working their cell phones for the greater part of the day. This has brought about a lack of involvement in homes, offices, and other spheres of life.

Involvement means to be actively present in the process of dialogue and not a passive presence. One can think of a passive presence in the scenario of a family gathered around the dinner table having a conversation, while someone at the same table has his/her hands under the table operating his/her phone and merely looking up at intervals to ask questions which may not tally with the flow of discussion. You may have also witnessed a situation where you are in dialogue with someone who, though physically present, is really far away in thought and lacks follow-up in whatever you may be saying.

In the chapter of this book that examined listening as an important aspect of dialogue, I asserted that active listening is a necessity in order to give the appropriate feedback that keeps the communication process going. In a situation where involvement is hampered because the other person is merely present physically, but absent-minded or preoccupied by his or her cell phone, dialogue cannot be said to be effective. As such, to rediscover authentic dialogue in human life, there is need to be fully involved in this process by avoiding every form of distraction and concentrating on the meaning that is being shared.

Interest: As lofty as the idea of involvement sounds, the context, content, and form of dialogue and many other factors are vital in either enhancing the interest or not of those engaged in this process. It is often said that people get more involved in things, activities, or people that satisfy their interest. As you read this book, think of an activity in which you have an interest and another in which you are forced to participate and evaluate your productivity in the two. You may notice that you put more effort into that activity in which you are interested. People tend to spend long hours of the day with friends rather than spend a minute with someone with whom they share no interest. Interest is an important aspect of the psychological make-up of a person, and it is important to employ the same towards enhancing the dialogue process.

In the communication process generally, and dialogue in particular, the display of interest should be reciprocal. That is, it should not be what only one party in the dialogue does while the other party maintains the indifference of a stoic. This stems from the fact that those in dialogue must value one another by developing shared interests that create more bonding experiences. The topic of dialogue should be tailored in a manner that interest is aroused and the mode of presentation should also be considered. You may have the best idea, but the way of presenting it to another person may put that other person off.

On the contrary, the worst idea may be presented in a way that people begin to see it as the best thing they ever heard. A typical example of a wrong presentation of a bright idea is that of the agent I talked about in the previous chapter of this book, who went from a culture where people write from left to right to present a medication to people who write from the right to left. An interesting topic coupled with interesting presentation increases the interest of people to engage in the process of dialogue. The onus is on both the initiator and receptor of the communication message to keep the interest up when engaged in dialogue.

The Golden Pause: The saying "Whoever fights to live, lives to fight another day" comes handy here. It is also often said that silence is golden. These sayings can be applied as a skill towards effective dialogue. This is because there are times when emotion is high among communicating persons, especially in a situation of conflict and, to continue dialoguing at this time may not be to a positive end. At such time, it may be advisable to take a pause and allow emotions to calm down. Given that time heals wounds, this may be what is needed to pick up dialogue at a later date, which will then bring about a better relationship between the communicating parties. While this pause is underway, it is important to leave open doors of communication, as to prolong the pause may be detrimental to the process of dialogue.

In essence, this chapter has focused on rediscovering the importance of dialogue in the present society. Building on everything I have said in preceding chapters, this chapter sums up the argument that every human person has inner dialogue, which I refer to as intra-personal discourse, from which all other forms of communication stem. The chapter looks at Pope Francis' letter for 2020 World Communications Day in which the issue of human interconnectedness was examined with the call for us to tell our stories in ways that build communities. This is the essence of communication in a real sense.

In sum, this chapter presents skills needed to engage in authentic dialogue, while at the same time affirming that dialogue is an ongoing process that oftentimes may result in conflicts. As such, ways of managing conflict were presented before examining ways to increase effectiveness in dialogue. In this concluding chapter, therefore, my aim has been to carry the reader along in this very important excursion into the fabric of human relationships, as I have endeavored to underscore how vital intra-personal discourse is to every other aspect of private relationships and public life. It is hoped that, backed by the thoughts, theories, and stories employed in this book, we will all give rightful place to intra-personal dialogue and, by so doing, bring about better, stronger, and enduring human relationships.

CONCLUSION

———————•———————

A number of years ago, when I was doing a Master's degree in Communication Studies, I went during my vacation to visit a senior priest. In the course of my visit, another friend of his came to spend some days with my host. While my host was introducing me to this other guest, he said jokingly, "This is Fr. Emmanuel – he is on vacation from school where he is studying communication. He is studying what I have been doing since I was a child." At this, they both burst out laughing. What was said jokingly that day has been a point of reflection for me over the years.

For many people, communication, dialogue, and in fact, anything that has to do with this discipline is often taken with a pinch of salt. People often feel communication is what we do every day, so, why do we need to study it again? While those who think like this are in one camp, there are others who have studied the science of communication and, with a deep understanding of what it entails, often ask if we really communicate as we should. For them, dialogue, which is an important aspect of communication, is easy to talk about but authentic dialogue is often difficult to accomplish.

My effort in this book has been to combine both forms of argument and, while not pretending to offer a synthesis of the duo, I have tried to show how important communication in general and dialogue in particular are to human relationships. Intra-personal dialogue, which has been singled out here, has been shown to be the fulcrum upon which hinges our day-to-day conversations. Like every other thing in nature that necessarily has a beginning, every form of human communication originates from an inner discourse with every person.

The thesis of this book has been to show that humans, knowingly or unknowingly, engage in an inner dialogue, which scholars call intra-personal dialogue and that this basic foundation of human communication has influence on other levels of communication – be it interpersonal, group, or organizational. All forms of communication in turn affect how we build, maintain, and foster relationships. Something as minute as making an eye contact can begin a conversation that can later lead to an enduring relationship.

As I mentioned in the third chapter of this book where I narrated my experience when studying in Rome, imagine what happens if you need to speak with someone who does not share your native language. Most times, we think in our native language before we express the idea in another language. What we do at this time is simply intra-personal dialogue. What we finally voice may appear simple and brilliant, but only the speaker knows the difficult task of intra-personal dialogue that went into play before such an idea is articulated. Apart from intra-personal dialogue in the example I just cited, I also had an experience in England, a number of years ago. At that time, while studying in Rome, during the summer vacation I worked as a supply priest in West London, England.

One day, a Spanish woman came to inquire something from the pastor of the church where I was serving. She did not understand a word of English, and the pastor knew no Spanish. He therefore called me to see if I could interpret from Spanish to English, since I speak Italian. It was not an easy task as I spoke to the woman in Italian, and she responded in Spanish; I then reported to the pastor in English and he, in turn, gave the feedback in English for me to inform the woman in Italian and for her to then respond in Spanish. The point here is that every dialogue has something similar to this experience, since many factors are involved in the process of communication. If the points laid out in the chapters of this book are taken into consideration, this task, which may seem difficult, becomes easy.

The theories I employed in the second chapter of this book, coupled with practical examples from 20 years of priestly ministry to people across various cultures, and my academic endeavor, show that humans go through similar experiences and that a better understanding of our realities should begin by the cognizance we give to our intra-personal dialogue. As I noted in the theoretical foundation for the book, the human person functions like a system in which every aspect is needed to maintain equilibrium. In the same vein, communicating persons must recognize the indispensable nature of everyone in the process of dialogue for it to be enduring. Although crises and conflicts may arise in human relationships, dialogue is the vehicle towards peaceful management of such situations.

As explained throughout this book, the need to constantly engage in dialogue was further underscored in the fourth chapter of this book where I narrated the experience of Jude, the young seminarian who came to a better understanding of himself by sharing with me his encounter with a senior student. Jude has since been ordained a Roman Catholic priest, but each time we see each other, he mentions how that experience in the seminary shaped his worldview and strengthened his faith in dialogue as a way of solving problems, no matter how difficult the situation may seem.

This experience of Jude is not the same as that of Mike and Mary, which I presented in chapter one of this book. Despite every effort by Mike to dialogue and resolve their marital challenge, Mary would not oblige him. In essence, not all dialogue issues may have a happy ending like that of Jude, but the fact that at least there is one like Jude's should further embolden one's faith in the power of dialogue. Even Mike who hitherto described himself as dialogue-doubter now claims to have an open mind towards dialogue. As such, the antidote to breakdown in dialogue is nothing else but dialogue.

This book does not pretend to have presented the final word on the issue of dialogue. If anything, like any academic endeavor, this is just the tip of the iceberg. Standing on the shoulders of scholars and practical experiences mentioned in this book, I have been able to see to a certain extent into the horizon, and it is hoped that this little effort will be of help to the readers as we all strive to bring about better relationships in our families, in offices, among friends, and in other aspects of life. As I mentioned earlier in this book, although the digital age has brought ease and immediacy to the communication process, relationship and communication through one-on-one facial dialogues, which give immediate feedback by showing the emotional, warmth, and cultural aspects of communication, help us to better understand the views of other people.

Suffice to note, a great deal of the misunderstanding presently ravaging our world (homes, offices, and nations) and personal relationships will be addressed, and lasting peace obtained, if people give the right place to understanding the importance of intra-personal dialogue and its influence on other forms of communication. This book has further shown that communication is like a web in which each aspect is linked with the others and, by not neglecting any aspect, we should take care of the whole. We are all caught up in a network of relationships, bound together by effective dialogue.

Conclusively, intra-personal dialogue is important as the basis for other forms of communication, and we should begin, more than ever before, to recognize this fact and let it guide our communication going forward. This might just be what we need to have a better understanding of ourselves as individuals, of our families, and of our world. The task of fostering relationships and achieving a better world starts within each of us – through intra-personal dialogue.

BIBLIOGRAPHY

———•———

Akintola, A. (1999). *Yoruba Ethics and Metaphysics*. Ibadan: Valour Publishing Ventures Limited.

Alexander, J. C. (2003). *The Meanings of Social Life: A Cultural Sociology*. New York: Oxford University Press.

Babatunde, E. D. (1992). *A Critical Study of Bini and Yoruba Value System of Nigeria in Change: Culture, Religion and the Self*. Wales, United Kingdom: The Edwin Mellen Press Limited.

Baraldi, Claudio, (2009). "Empowering Dialogue in Intercultural Settings" in C. Baraldi (Ed.) *Dialogue in Intercultural Communities* (pp. 3-27). Philadelphia: John Benjamins Publishing Company.

Baron R. A. & Branscombe, N. R. (2014). *Social Psychology*. 13th Edition. London: Pearson.

Beller, R. (2001). *Life, Person and Community in Africa: A Way Towards Inculturation with the Spirituality of the Focolare*. Nairobi: Pauline Publications Africa.

Birdwhistell, Ray L. (1955). "Background to Kinesics". *Review of General Semantics*, vol. 13, 10-18.

Birdwhistell, Ray L. (1991). "A Kinesic-Linguistic Exercise: The Cigarette Scene", in J. Gumperz, & D. Hymes (Eds.), *Directions in Sociolinguistics: The Ethnography of Communication* (pp. 381-404). Oxford: Willey-Blackwell.

Bormann, E. G. (2003). "Symbolic Convergence Theory", in R. Hirokawa, R. Cathcart, L. Samovar, and L. Henman (Eds.), *Small Group Communication: Theory and Practice* (pp. 39-40). California: Roxbury Publishing Company.

Bourgault, L. M. (1995). *Mass Media in Sub-Saharan Africa.* Indianapolis: Indiana University Press.

Boyd, B. M. & Ellison, N. B. (2007). "Social Network Sites: Definition, History and Scholarship". *Journal of Computer-Mediated Communication,* 13(1), 1-11.

Boyd, D. (2007). "None of this is Real: Identity and Participation in Friendster", in J. Karaganis, (Ed.), *Structures of Participation in Digital Culture* (pp. 132-157). New York: Social Science Research Council.

Boyd, D. (2008). "Why Youth Social Network Sites: The Role of Networked Publics in Teenage Social Life" in D. Buckingham (Ed.), *Youth Identity and Digital Media, The John D and Catherine T. MacArthur Foundation Series on Digital Media and Learning* (pp. 199-142). Cambridge, MA: The MIT Press.

Brooks, M. (2005). "Drawing as a Unique Mental Development Tool for Young Children: Interpersonal and Intra-personal Dialogues". *Contemporary Issues in Early Childhood,*
vol. 6(1), 80-91.

Cacioppo, J. T., Gardner, W. L. & Bernstson, G. G. (1999). "The Affect System Has Parallel and Integrative Processing Components: Form follows Function". *Journal of Personality and Social Psychology,* 76(5), 839-855.

Chen, G. M. (2011). "Tweet This: A Uses and Gratifications Perspective on How Active Twitter Use Gratifies a Need to Connect with Others". *Computer in Human Behaviors,* 27(2), 755-762.

Clarke, T. J., Bradshaw, M. F., Field, D. T., Hampson, S. E., & Rose, D. (2005). "The Perception of Emotion from Body Movement in Point-Light Displays of Interpersonal Dialogue". *Perception,* 34(10), 1171–1180. https://doi.org/10.1068/p5203 accessed on Jan. 27, 2020.

Coello, Y. & Fischer, M. (2015). "Embodied Perception of Objects and People in Space: Towards a Unified Theoretical Framework", in Y. Coello & M. Fischer (Eds.), *Foundations of Embodied Cognition* (pp. 198-219). New York: Psychology Press.

Connors, J. V. (2011). "Systems Theory and Interpersonal Relationships", in J. V. Connors, *Interpersonal Peacemaking Reader* (pp. 309-324). San Diego: University Readers.

Crush, J. (1995). "Introduction: Imagining Development", in J. Crush (Ed.), *Power of Development,* London: Routledge.

Fisher, D. & Harms, L. S. (Eds.) (1982). *The Right to Communicate: A New Human Right.* Dublin: Boole Press.

Francis, (2019). "A Document on Human Fraternity for World Peace and Living Together" http://www.vatican.va/content/francesco/en/travels/2019/outside/documents/papa-francesco_20190204_documento-fratellanza-umana.html

Francis, (2020). "Fratelli Tutti – Encyclical Letter on Fraternity and Social Friendship" http://www.vatican.va/content/francesco/en/encyclicals/documents/papa-francesco 20201003 enciclica-fratelli-tutti.html

Francis, (2020). "Peace as a Journey of Hope: Dialogue, Reconciliation and Ecological Conversion", Message for the Celebration of 53rd World Day of Peace, http:www.vatican.va, accessed January 12, 2020.

Francis, (2020). "That You May Tell Your Children and Grandchildren (Ex. 10:2): Life Becomes History", Message for 54th World Communications Day, http:www.zenith.org, accessed May 22, 2020.

Freire, P. (1981). *Education for Critical Consciousness*, New York: Continuum Publishing Corporation.

Gbadegesin, S. (1991). *African Philosophy: Traditional Yoruba Philosophy and Contemporary Realities*. London: Peter Lang.

Geiman, K. L. & Greene, J. O. (2019). "Listening and Experiences of Interpersonal Transcendence". *Communication Studies*, 70(1), 114-128.

Giddens, A. (2001). *Sociology*. 4th ed. Cambridge: Polity Press.

Gouran, D. S. (1999). "Communication in Groups: The Emergence and Evolution of a Field of Study", in L. R. Frey, D. S. Gouran & M. S. Poole (Eds.) *The Handbook of Group Communication Theory and Research* (pp. 3-36). London: Sage Publications.

Graham D. B. (2011). "The Understudied Nature of Listening in Interpersonal Communication: Introduction to a Special Issue". *International Journal of Listening*, 25(1&2), 1-9.

Greece, A. K. (2014). "What Types of Learning May Occur through Casual Use of Social Network Site: The Case of Facebook". *Online Journal of Media and Communication Technology*, 4(2), 170-211.

Hall, E. (1963). "A System for the Notation of Proxemic Behavior". *American Anthropologist*, 1003-1026.

Hall, E. (1976). *Beyond Culture*. New York: Anchor Press.

Hamelink, D. J. (2003). "Grounding the Human Right to Communicate" in P. Lee (Ed.), *Many Voices One Vision: The Right to Communicate in Practice* (pp. 21-31). London: Southbound Penang.

Hays, S. (2000). "Constructing the Centrality of Culture and Deconstructing Sociology". *Contemporary Sociology*, 29, 594-602.

Heil, A. (2020). *Systems Theory* SPC 330. www.siue.edu accessed January 10, 2020.

Isaacs, W. (2010). *Dialogue and the Art of Thinking Together: A Pioneering Approach to Communicating in Business and Life.* New York: Currency.

Jolly, S. (2000). "Understanding Body Language: Birdwhistell's Theory of Kinesics". *Corporate Communications: An International Journal,* 5(3), 133-139.

Katz, E., Blumler, J. G. & Gurevitch, M. (1974). "Utilization of Mass Communication by Individual", in J. G. Blumler & E. Katz (Eds.), *The Uses of Mass Communication: Current Perspectives on Gratifications Research* (pp. 19-31). Beverly Hills: Sage Publications.

Kellner, D. (1992). "Popular Culture and the Construction of Postmodern Identities", in S. Lash & J. Friedman (Eds.), *Modernity and Identity* (pp. 141-177). Oxford: Blackwell.

Kennedy, D. P., Tyszka, J. M., Glascher, J. P. & Adolphs, R. (2009). "Personal Space Regulation by the Human Amygdala". *Nature Neuroscience,* 12(10), 1226-7.

Kim, W. L. (2004). "Malaysia Women in the Information Society: Opportunities and Challenges", in P. Lee (Ed.), *Many Voices One Vision: The Right to Communicate in Practice* (pp. 119-131). London: Southbound Penang.

Kleinwachter, W. (1995). "Is There a Need for the Right to Communicate in Cyberspace?" *Javnost* (The Public), 2(1), 107-131.

Kocak, D. O. (2013). "The Lack of Collective Memory and Identity Construction in Cyberspace". *Online Journal of Media and Communication Technology,* 3(2), 203-226.

Koonin, M. (2013). "Management Risk, Reputation and Identity of Young Adults in a Social Environment". *Online Journal of Communication and Media Technology,* 3(2), 75-94.

Kwon, O. & Wen, Y. (2010). "An Empirical Study of the Factors Affecting Social Network Service Use". *Computers in Human Behavior,* 26, 254-263.

Ladele, T. A., Aworinde, I. A., Oyebamiji, M., Olatubosun, O., Oyedemi, O. & Afolabi, O. (1986). *Akojopo Iwadii Ijinle Asa Yoruba.* Ibadan: Macmillan Nigeria Publishers Limited.

Lasswell, H. (1948). "The Structure and Function of Communication in Society", in L. Bryson, (Ed.), *The Communication of Ideas* (pp. 37-51). New York: Harper & Row Publishers.

Lewis, P. M. (2002). "Radio Theory and Community Radio", in N. W. Jankowski & O. Prehn (Eds.), *Community Media in the Information Age: Perspectives and Prospects* (pp. 47-61). New Jersey: Hampton Press Inc.

Marwick, A. & Boyd, D. (2011). "I Tweet Honestly, I Tweet Passionately: Twitter Users, Context Collapse and the Imagined Audience". *New Media and Society,* 13(1), 114-133.

Milkie, M. A. & Denny, K. E. (2014). "Changes in the Cultural Model of Father Involvement: Descriptions of Benefits to Fathers, Children, and Mothers in Parents' Magazine, 1926-2006". *Journal of Family Issues,* vol. 35(2), 223-253.

Mitsztal, B. A. (2003). *Theories of Social Remembering.* Maidenhead, Philadelphia: Open University Press.

Mowlana, H. (2018). "On Human Communication". *The Public,* vol. 25, Nos. 1–2, 226–232, https://doi.org/10.1080/13183222.2018.1418978

Mumbengegwi, C. (1986). "Continuity and Change in Agricultural Policy", in I. Mandaza (Ed.), *Zimbabwe – The Political Economy of Transition* (pp. 203-222). Harare: Jogwe Press.

Nixon, P. (2012). *Dialogue Gap: Why Communication Isn't Enough and What We Can Do About It, Fast.* Singapore: John Wiley & Sons Singapore Pte. Limited.

Nordenstreng, K. (1984). *The Mass Media Declaration of UNESCO*. New Jersey: Ablex
Publishing Corporation.

Ogundimu, F. F. (2017). "Media and Democracy in Twenty-First-Century Africa", in G. Hyden,

M. Leslie & F. F. Ogundimu, *Media and Democracy in Africa* (pp. 207-238). New York: Routledge.

Olusola, E. B. (2012). "Merits and Demerits of Information and Communication Technology (ICT) for Users of the New Media in Nigeria". *Journal of Inculturation Theology*, 13(2), 227-244.

Pavitt, C. (1999). "Theorizing About the Group Communication-Leadership Relationship: Input-

Process-Output and Functional Models", in L. R. Frey (Ed.), *The Handbook of Group*

Communication Theory and Research (pp. 313-334). London: Sage Publications.

Poole, M. S. (1999). "Group Communication Theory", in L. R. Frey, D. S. Gouran & M. S. Poole, (Eds.), *The Handbook of Group Communication Theory and Research* (pp. 37-91). London: Sage Publications.

Richstad, J. (2003). "Right to Communicate in the Internet Age", in C. J. Bertrand (Ed.), *An Arsenal for Democracy: Media Accountability Systems* (pp. 35-48). New Jersey: Hampton Press Inc.

Rogers, E. M. (1986). *Communication Technology: The New Media in Society*. New York: The Free Press.

Rose, G. (2016). "Cultural Geography Going Viral". *Social & Cultural Geography*, 17(6), 763-767.

Rose-Redwood, R., Kitchin, R., Rickards, L., Rossi, U., Datta, A. & Crampton, J. (2018). "The Possibilities and Limits to Dialogue". *Dialogues in Human Geography*, vol. 8(2), 109-123.

Saxena, P. (2015). "JOHARI WINDOW: An Effective Model for Improving Interpersonal Communication and Managerial Effectiveness". *SIT Journal of Management*, vol. 5(2), 134-146.

Servaes, J. (2004). "Human Rights, Participatory Communication and Cultural Freedom", in P. Lee, (Ed.), *Many Voices One Vision: The Right to Communicate in Practice* (pp. 150-165). London: Southbound Penang.

Shownberger, H. & Tandoc, E. (2014). "Updated Statuses: Understanding Facebook Use through Explicit and Implicit Measures of Attitudes and Motivations". *Online Journal of Communication and Media Technology*, 4(1), 217-244.

Sommer, R. (2002). "Personal Space in a Digital Age", in R. B. Bechtel & A. Churchman (Eds.), *Handbook of Environmental Psychology* (647-660). Oxford: John Wiley.

Spranzi, M. (2011). *The Art of Dialectic between Dialogue and Rhetoric: The Aristotelian Tradition*. Philadelphia: John Benjamins Publishing Company.

Stacks, D., Hickson, M. and Hill, S. (1991). *Introduction to Communication Theory*. London: Holt, Rinehart and Winston, Inc.

Step, M. M. & Finucane, M. O. (2002). "Interpersonal Communication Motives in Everyday Interactions". *Communication Quarterly*, vol. 50(1), 93-109.

Swidler, A. (1986). "Culture in Action: Symbols and Strategies". *American Sociological Review*, 51, 273-286.

Taiwo, R. (2010). "The Thumb Tribe: Creativity and Social Change through SMS in Nigeria". *California Linguistic Notes*, 35(1), 1-17.

Tella, A., Adetoro, N. & Adekunle, P. A. (2009). "A Case Study of the Global System of Mobile Communication (GSM) in Nigeria". *The European Journal for the Informatics Professional*, 10(2), 54-59.

Thomas, P., (1994). "Participatory Development Communication: Philosophical Premises@, in White, S., Nair, K.S., Ascroftl, J. (Eds.), Participatory Communication: Working for Social Change and Development, (49-59). New Delhi: Sage Publications.

Trager, G. L. (1961). "The Typology of Paralanguage". *Anthropological Linguistics*, vol. 3(1), 17-21.

Turkle, S. (1995). *Life on the Screen: Identity in the Age of the Internet*. London: Simon and Schuster.

Turner, L. H. & West, R. (2002). *Perspectives on Family Communication* (2nd ed.). Boston: McGraw-Hill.

Van Djick, J. (2013). *The Culture of Connectivity: A Critical History of Social Media*. New York: Oxford University Press.

Weizman, E. (2008). *Positioning in Media Dialogue*. Amsterdam & Philadelphia: John Benjamins Publishing Company.

White, R. (1995). "Democratization of Communication as a Social Movement Process", in P. Lee(Ed.), *The Democratization of Communication*, (92-113). Cardiff: University of Wales Press.

INDEX

Printed in Canada